Magento 2 Development Essentials

Get up and running with Magento 2 to create custom
solutions, themes, and extensions effectively

Fernando J. Miguel

BIRMINGHAM - MUMBAI

Magento 2 Development Essentials

First published: February 2016

Production reference: 1220216

Published by Packt Publishing Ltd.
Livery Place
35 Livery Street
Birmingham B3 2PB, UK.

ISBN 978-1-78528-989-7

www.packtpub.com

Credits

Author
Fernando J. Miguel

Reviewers
Michel Arteta
Miguel I. Balparda
Clive Walkden

Commissioning Editor
Veena Pagare

Acquisition Editor
Larissa Pinto

Content Development Editor
Sanjeet Rao

Technical Editor
Anushree Arun Tendulkar

Copy Editor
Shruti Iyer

Project Coordinator
Judie Jose

Proofreader
Safis Editing

Indexer
Tejal Soni Daruwale

Graphics
Jason Monteiro

Production Coordinator
Manu Joseph

Cover Work
Manu Joseph

About the Author

Fernando J. Miguel is a certified professional scrum master at the Scrum Alliance, with experience in analysis and web application development since 2003. He has been working in project development using design patterns, MVC, object-oriented programming, and Agile. He also has experience with content management systems (CMS), WordPress, Joomla, Magento 2, PHP, Java, Node.js, Android, SQL, NoSQL, and cloud computing.

Fernando has a bachelor's degree in information systems from Centro Universitário Módulo, Brazil. He specializes in project management / PMI-PMBOK from Universidade Cruzeiro do Sul, Brazil. He also specializes in health informatics from Universidade Federal de São Paulo, Brazil, and he is currently pursuing a master's degree in electronic engineering and computer informatics from Instituto de Tecnologia e Aeronáutica (ITA), one of the best technology institutes in Brazil.

I'd like to thank my great professors, masters, and references Adilson Marques da Cunha, Flávio Marques Azevedo, and Renato Vercesi Mader for the valuable teachings and professional experience contribution, which enabled the building of this project.

About the Reviewers

Michel Arteta is a Magento-certified frontend developer, currently working as a frontend developer at Dow Jones (Innovation Department, Web and Mobile Development), New York. With more than 5 years of experience in web development, Michel has a strong background in modern web application development. He currently lives in New York and can be contacted on Twitter at @michelarteta.

Previously, he has worked for Faro Group, Founder (Magento Development) and Nano Web Group (Magento Development) in New York.

> I would love to thank to my father, mother, and the woman I love, for her unconditional love and support.

Miguel I. Balparda is a Magento developer, speaker, Linux aficionado, and full-time traveler.

Clive Walkden is a PHP developer with a passion for learning, constantly looking at open source frameworks to improve his knowledge of coding. His favorite frameworks currently are Magento and Laravel.

Clive has over 15 years of programming experience. For the last 5 years, he has been the lead developer at SOZO Design, an agency in Cheltenham, UK, that focuses on PHP/SQL websites of all sizes from brochures to international e-commerce websites.

I'd like to thank the author for taking the time to write a book on how to get started building a website using Magento. It's not an easy task, and this book accomplishes this very well. Packt, for their confidence in my knowledge and experience to approach me as a technical reviewer. I would finally also like to thank my family and friends for their support and encouragement.

www.PacktPub.com

eBooks, discount offers, and more

Did you know that Packt offers eBook versions of every book published, with PDF and ePub files available? You can upgrade to the eBook version at www.PacktPub.com and as a print book customer, you are entitled to a discount on the eBook copy. Get in touch with us at customercare@packtpub.com for more details.

At www.PacktPub.com, you can also read a collection of free technical articles, sign up for a range of free newsletters and receive exclusive discounts and offers on Packt books and eBooks.

https://www2.packtpub.com/books/subscription/packtlib

Do you need instant solutions to your IT questions? PacktLib is Packt's online digital book library. Here, you can search, access, and read Packt's entire library of books.

Why subscribe?

- Fully searchable across every book published by Packt
- Copy and paste, print, and bookmark content
- On demand and accessible via a web browser

To my grandmother, Mildes, and my mother, Edneia, wherever they are,
I'm sure they are very happy with my work. To my beloved wife, Elizabete,
for the countless hours of patience with my work.
Love you.

Table of Contents

Preface

Digital buyers are improving economies around the world, and information technology (IT) provides the necessary subsides to allow customers to buy services and products over the Internet. According to the research conducted by Statista (`http://goo.gl/BSCiuO`), in 2016, 1.12 billion people worldwide are expected to buy goods and services online.

Since the launch of `Amazon.com`, the first commercial-free 24-hour e-commerce website, the universe of software development techniques has evolved, and new approaches are emerging, such as cloud computing—previously no more than an embryonic idea, today a concrete application.

The Magento Commerce company, recognized as the leading e-commerce platform in the 2015 Internet Retailer Top 1000, B2B 300, and Hot 100 lists, is in constant evolution since the first Magento Community Edition (CE) system version in 2008. Launched recently, Magento CE 2.0 has great features and takes advantage of the newest client-server techniques providing a mature e-commerce system and a promising professional area to explore.

Magento, used by thousands of merchants for their transactions worth billions, provides the flexibility to customize the content and functionality of your website. By strengthening your fundamentals in Magento development, you can develop the best solutions and take advantage of the growing market.

This fast-paced tutorial will provide you with skills you need to successfully create themes, extensions, and solutions to Magento 2 projects.

This book begins by showing you how to set up Magento 2 before gradually moving onto setting the basic options of the Sell System. You will take advantage of Search Engine Optimization aspects, create design and customize theme layout, develop new extensions, and adjust the Magento System to achieve great performance. By the end of the book, you will have quickly explored all the features of Magento 2 to create a great solution.

With ample examples and a practical approach, this book will ensure your success with this astonishing e-commerce management system.

Enjoy the read.

What this book covers

Chapter 1, Magento Fundamentals, teaches you how to create a basic environment, install Magento 2.0, and study some Magento concepts.

Chapter 2, Magento 2.0 Features, helps you discover the features of Magento 2.0 and configure some basic Magento options.

Chapter 3, Working with Search Engine Optimization, provides you with some configuration tips to tweak the Magento options for SEO purposes.

Chapter 4, Magento 2.0 Theme Development – the Developers' Holy Grail, gives you an overview of theme development and techniques of customizing Magento 2.0.

Chapter 5, Creating a Responsive Magento 2.0 Theme, implements a practical project to create your custom theme.

Chapter 6, Write Magento 2.0 Extensions – a Great Place to Go, provides you with development techniques by implementing a practical project to create your own Magento extension.

Chapter 7, Go Mobile with Magento 2.0!, covers techniques of working with Magento on mobile devices.

Chapter 8, Speeding up Your Magento 2.0, explains good practices to fine-tune your Magento system and environment to gain performance.

Chapter 9, Improving Your Magento Skills, explores the tools and ways to improve your skills in the Magento universe.

What you need for this book

You need the following for the projects in this book:

Operating Systems:

- Linux, OSX or Windows (7, 8 or 10);

Software:

- XAMPP
- Browser (Google Chrome or Firefox)
- Code editor (Sublime Text, Notepad++ or Atom.io)

Who this book is for

If you are a PHP developer who wants to improve your skills in e-commerce development by creating themes and extensions for Magento 2, then this book is for you.

Conventions

In this book, you will find a number of text styles that distinguish between different kinds of information. Here are some examples of these styles and an explanation of their meaning.

Code words in text, database table names, folder names, filenames, file extensions, pathnames, dummy URLs, user input, and Twitter handles are shown as follows: "In order to start XAMPP for Windows, you can execute `xampp-control.exe`."

A block of code is set as follows:

```
<theme xmlns:xsi="http://www.w3.org/2001/XMLSchema-instance" xsi:noNam
espaceSchemaLocation="urn:magento:framework:Config/etc/theme.xsd">
    <title>Magento Luma</title>
    <parent>Magento/blank</parent>
    <media>
        <preview_image>media/preview.jpg</preview_image>
    </media>
</theme>
```

When we wish to draw your attention to a particular part of a code block, the relevant lines or items are set in bold:

```
<Magento root directory>/app/design/frontend/Packt
```

Any command-line input or output is written as follows:

```
<Magento root directory>/app/design/frontend/Packt/basic
```

New terms and **important words** are shown in bold. Words that you see on the screen, for example, in menus or dialog boxes, appear in the text like this: "Complete the installation by pressing the **Finish** button."

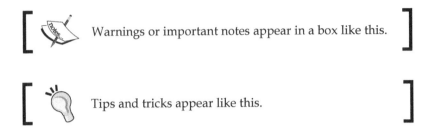

Warnings or important notes appear in a box like this.

Tips and tricks appear like this.

Reader feedback

Feedback from our readers is always welcome. Let us know what you think about this book—what you liked or disliked. Reader feedback is important for us as it helps us develop titles that you will really get the most out of.

To send us general feedback, simply e-mail feedback@packtpub.com, and mention the book's title in the subject of your message.

If there is a topic that you have expertise in and you are interested in either writing or contributing to a book, see our author guide at www.packtpub.com/authors.

Customer support

Now that you are the proud owner of a Packt book, we have a number of things to help you to get the most from your purchase.

Downloading the example code

You can download the example code files for this book from your account at http://www.packtpub.com. If you purchased this book elsewhere, you can visit http://www.packtpub.com/support and register to have the files e-mailed directly to you.

You can download the code files by following these steps:

1. Log in or register to our website using your e-mail address and password.
2. Hover the mouse pointer on the **SUPPORT** tab at the top.
3. Click on **Code Downloads & Errata**.

4. Enter the name of the book in the **Search** box.

5. Select the book for which you're looking to download the code files.

6. Choose from the drop-down menu where you purchased this book from.

7. Click on **Code Download**.

Once the file is downloaded, please make sure that you unzip or extract the folder using the latest version of:

- WinRAR / 7-Zip for Windows
- Zipeg / iZip / UnRarX for Mac
- 7-Zip / PeaZip for Linux

Downloading the color images of this book

We also provide you with a PDF file that has color images of the screenshots/ diagrams used in this book. The color images will help you better understand the changes in the output. You can download this file from `http://www.packtpub. com/sites/default/files/downloads/Magento_Development_By_Example_ ColoredImages.pdf`.

Errata

Although we have taken every care to ensure the accuracy of our content, mistakes do happen. If you find a mistake in one of our books—maybe a mistake in the text or the code—we would be grateful if you could report this to us. By doing so, you can save other readers from frustration and help us improve subsequent versions of this book. If you find any errata, please report them by visiting `http://www.packtpub. com/submit-errata`, selecting your book, clicking on the **Errata Submission Form** link, and entering the details of your errata. Once your errata are verified, your submission will be accepted and the errata will be uploaded to our website or added to any list of existing errata under the Errata section of that title.

To view the previously submitted errata, go to `https://www.packtpub.com/books/ content/support` and enter the name of the book in the search field. The required information will appear under the **Errata** section.

Piracy

Piracy of copyrighted material on the Internet is an ongoing problem across all media. At Packt, we take the protection of our copyright and licenses very seriously. If you come across any illegal copies of our works in any form on the Internet, please provide us with the location address or website name immediately so that we can pursue a remedy.

Please contact us at copyright@packtpub.com with a link to the suspected pirated material.

We appreciate your help in protecting our authors and our ability to bring you valuable content.

Questions

If you have a problem with any aspect of this book, you can contact us at questions@packtpub.com, and we will do our best to address the problem.

1
Magento Fundamentals

Magento is a highly customizable e-commerce platform and content management system. Magento is one of the most used e-commerce systems to create online stores around the world by providing management of inventory, orders, customers, payments, and much more. It has a powerful scalable architecture.

Are you ready to start on the world of Magento development?

First of all, we will need to set up our environment. In this book, we will cover how to set up a local environment. It is very important to have this local ecosystem development to work smoothly and in an agile way.

In every chapter of this book, we will work with a mini project. It's kind of a sprint to learn the path. In this chapter, our mission is to create a work environment and understand the basic concepts of Magento (`http://magento.com/`).

After setting up the environment, you'll study the Magento folder structure and work on a basic **Model View Controller** (**MVC**) software architecture pattern and Magento basic setup.

Basically, we will work on this chapter with the following topics:

- XAMPP PHP development environment
- Magento e-commerce system
- Magento system structure
- Magento basic setup

Are you ready for fun some? Let's go!

XAMPP PHP development environment

The **XAMPP** is a complete web development environment. On its install package, we can find **Apache**, **MySQL**, **PHP**, and **Perl**. This is everything that you will want to develop your solutions!

At this time, you can imagine the meaning of XAMPP, but the **X** before the AMPP has the meaning of cross or cross-platform. So, we have XAMMP: (**X**) Cross-platform, **Apache**, **Maria** DB, PHP, and Perl.

The goal of XAMPP is to build an easy-to-install distribution for developers to get into the world of Apache. XAMPP is a project of **Apache Friends** (Apache Friends is a non-profit project to promote the Apache web server).

Why we are working with this software? Let's find out:

- **Apache** (http://httpd.apache.org/): This has been the most popular web server on the Internet since April 1995 providing secure, efficient, and extensible HTTP services in sync with the current HTTP standards
- **MariaDB** (https://mariadb.org/): This strives to be the logical choice for database professionals looking for a robust, scalable, and reliable SQL server
- **PHP** (http://php.net/): This is a popular general-purpose scripting language that is especially suited to web development; and, most importantly, it is the main language of Magento
- **Perl** (https://www.perl.org/): This is a highly capable, feature-rich programming language with over 27 years of development

So far so good, but how about doing some action?

XAMPP installation

First of all, let's access the XAMPP website on `https://www.apachefriends.org/`.

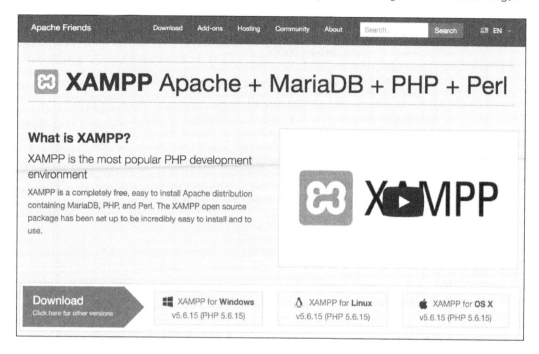

XAMPP has three distinct versions for different **operating systems (OS)**: Windows, Linux, and OS X. Choose your preferred version to download, and start the installation process.

XAMPP for Windows installation

XAMPP for Windows has three different kinds of installation files:

- **Installer**: This is a classic Windows installation method
- **Zip**: This method uses compressed files to install manually
- **7zip**: This method uses compressed files to install manually

The (.exe) installer is the most popular process to install. Download it and execute to start the installation process, shown as follows:

1. You can skip FileZilla FTP Server, Mercury Mail Server, and Tomcat for our installation purposes but feel free to consult **Apache Friends Support Forum** for further information at https://community.apachefriends.org.

2. On XAMPP, we have the option to use **Bitnami** (https://bitnami.com/ xampp), but for learning purposes, we will install Magento in a classic way.

3. Complete the installation by pressing the **Finish** button.

4. In order to start XAMPP for Windows, you can execute `xampp-control.exe` and start the **Apache** web server.

5. To test if everything is working, type `http://localhosturl` in your favorite web browser. You will see the XAMPP start page:

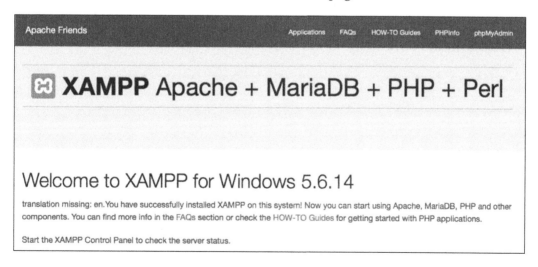

XAMPP for Linux installation

XAMPP for Linux has two main versions of installation files:

- 32-bit version
- 64-bit version

Choose the file according to your architecture and follow these steps:

1. Change the permissions to the installer:

   ```
   chmod 755 xampp-linux-*-installer.run
   ```

2. Run the installer:

   ```
   sudo ./xampp-linux-*-installer.run
   ```

   XAMPP is now installed below the /opt/lampp directory.

3. To start XAMPP, execute this command on terminal:

   ```
   sudo /opt/lampp/lampp start
   ```

4. To test if everything is working, type the http://localhost URL in your favorite web browser. You will see the XAMPP start page:

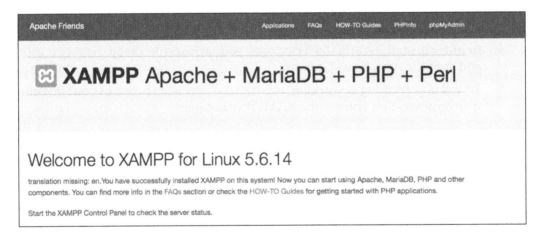

XAMPP for OS X installation

To install XAMPP for OS X, you simply need to follow these steps:

1. Download the DMG image file.

2. Open the image file to start the installation process.

3. The steps are pretty much the same as Windows installation.

4. To test if everything is working, type the `http://localhost` URL in your favorite web browser. You will see the XAMPP start page:

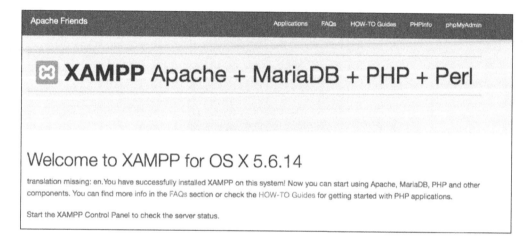

The XAMPP `htdocs` folder is the *docroot* folder of your server. Everything that you save on `htdocs` can be accessed via any browser. For example, if you save `index.php` inside the `htdocs` root, you can access this script by entering `http://localhost/index.php`. If you save your file in the `packt` folder, you can access it by `http://localhost/packt/index.php`. Piece of cake!

Magento

Magento is an open source content management system for e-commerce websites. It's one of the most important e-commerce systems, which has grown fast since its launch in 2008.

Basically, Magento works with two different types of Magento: **Community Edition** (**CE**) and **Enterprise Edition** (**EE**). In this book, we will cover CE.

On a study provided by aheadWorks (`https://aheadworks.com/`) in October 2014, Magento CE has taken the leading position among examined e-commerce platforms.

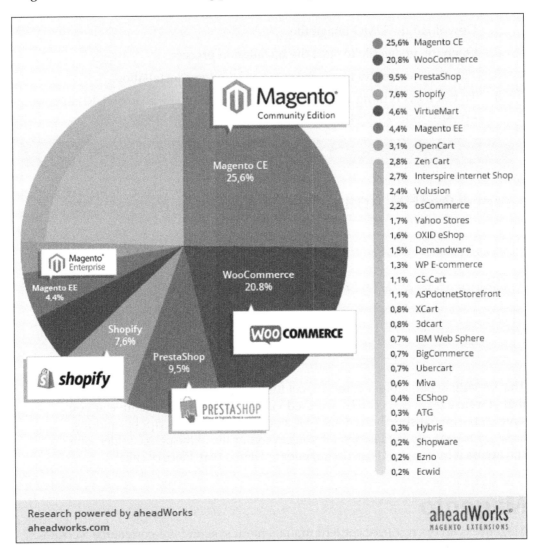

Now, we have solid concepts about "where we are going". It's very important to have solids concepts about every aspect that you are working on in this moment. Globally, e-commerce shows a remarkable potential market and Magento professionals are welcome.

Magento installation

First of all, we need to create a user account on the Magento website (`http://www.magento.com`) to download Magento CE. Click on the top-menu link **My Account** and after clicking the button labeled **Register**, fill out the form and confirm your registration.

Once registered, you gain access to download Magento CE. You can access the **Products | Open Source/CE** and **VIEW AVAILABLE DOWNLOADS** menus.

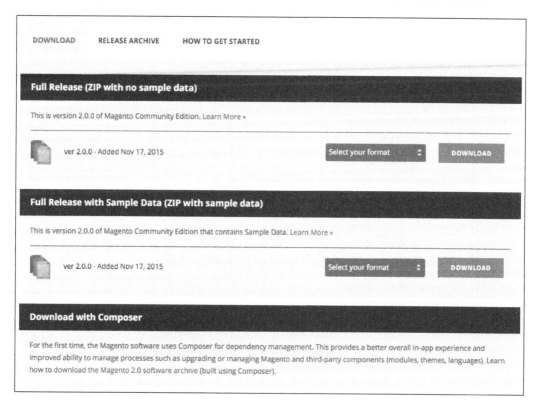

On this page, we have three important options:

- **Full Release (ZIP with no sample data)**: This is a complete download of the last and stable Magento version

- **Full Release with Sample Data (ZIP with sample data)**: This is important to create example products to our store for testing.

- **Download with Composer**: This is the dependency management installation tool

Choose the **Full Release with Sample Data (ZIP with sample data)** option for downloading Magento. Extract the compressed files in the XAMPP `htdocsfolder` and rename the folder to `packt`.

 Remember to start Apache and MySQL services on the XAMPP panel before the installation.

Before starting the Magento installation, we'll need to create a new MySQL database instance to store the Magento data. **phpMyAdmin** is a MySQL web app to manage your database and can be accessed at `http://localhost/phpmyadmin/`.

Click on the **Databases** menu and the **Create database** option to create the `packt` database.

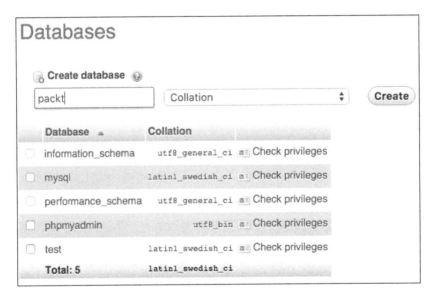

Now, let's start our Magento installation. On your browser, access `http://localhost/packt/setup`.

By now, you will see this installation page on your browser:

Let's start the Magento installation by following these steps:

1. **Readiness Check**: Check the environment for the correct PHP version, PHP extensions, file permissions, and compatibility.

2. **Add a Database**: Fill the database form with your connection information. By default, you can follow the suggestions given here:

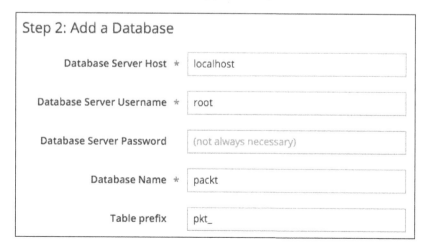

3. **Web Configuration**: Enter you store address and admin address here:

4. **Customize Your Store**: In this step you provide the time zone, currency, and language information:

5. **Create an Admin Account**: Enter with personal login information and set the admin address to `packt-admin`.

After all these steps, we are done! Congratulations! We have our first Magento installation!

You can access your new site by accessing the URL at `http://localhost/packt`:

And you can access the admin area by accessing the URL at `http://localhost/`
`packt/admin-packt`:

For more information about Magento installation, access `http://devdocs.`
`magento.com/guides/v2.0/install-gde/bk-install-guide.html`.

Magento MVC architecture

MVC is an architectural software pattern that works with three different but
interconnected parts. Its principal mission is to abstract the development work
into interdependent layers providing the best practices to documentation and
organization of software projects.

The Magento e-commerce solution is written with the PHP **Zend** framework,
which is one of the most powerful PHP frameworks. For more information,
access `http://framework.zend.com/`.

Magento is a *configuration-based* MVC System. For example, when you develop a module (we will check this in the next chapters), besides creating new files and classes to your module, you need to also create a `config.xml` file. This file contains all the configuration data for Magento module. These practices abstract some important information that you can easily edit to set the module as you need.

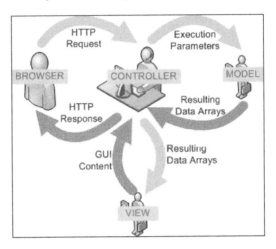

In this book, we will cover only the very basic Magento software architecture concepts, but it's highly recommended that you to study more software design patterns, especially in our case MVC software architecture needs to be understood well to best experience the field of software development.

Summary

You've now seen what Magento can do; you have installed Magento too. You started to understand the basic concepts of Magento, and certainly, you'll get more experience in developing your own Magento solutions by working in the projects of this book.

In the next chapter, we'll work with some Magento Sell System features.

2
Magento 2.0 Features

Magento has many features to provide a great experience to the users and developers. Understanding what Magento can provide is the key to success in the development of Magento. All Magento developers seek for improvements in this area.

On the Magento Connect site (`https://www.magentocommerce.com/magento-connect/`), you can search for uncountable extensions to improve your Magento solution: `Checkout`, `Cart`, `Order Management`, `Gifting`, `Pricing`, and `Promotion`, and a lot more. At this point, it is crucial to understand that Magento has a native solution and how its features can help you think of some great solutions for development.

In the previous chapter, you learned the fundamentals to create a basic local Magento environment to work with book projects. In this chapter, you will learn how Magento manages and improves system sell processes.

The following topics will be covered in this chapter:

- Magento features
- Magento architecture
- Magento order management
- Magento command-line utility configurations

Have fun!

The revolution of Magento 2.0

Magento Commerce has promoted important changes between its 1.x and 2.0 versions. Some usual problems of the Magento 1.x version were fixed in this new version. The following processes/modules have received improvements in Magento 2.0:

- Performance
- Payment method
- Checkout
- Catalog
- CMS
- Web API
- Framework
- Setup

All good software or systems pass through incremental improvements for evolving according to its production environment; it couldn't be different with a commerce platform that powers over 250,000 online stores worldwide.

Magento 2.0 CE has a flexible architecture and a modular code base; it has a modern theming and an extensive **Application Programming Interface (API)**. To get a better performance, Magento 2.0 compresses JavaScript files and images and gives support to **Apache Varnish** integration on the server side to enable faster performance.

Security is another subject treated in the Magento 2.0 system. According to its official documentation (`http://goo.gl/E7sPm3`), Magento 2.0 has had substantial enhancements in its security layer:

- Enhanced password management
- An improved prevention of cross-site scripting (XSS)
- Restricted permissions for file access
- An improved prevention of click jacking exploits
- The use of non-default admin URL

Extensibility and modularity allow Magento to be highly customizable. As an objected-oriented solution, Magento follows good architectural principles and coding standards that provide *high cohesion* and *loose coupling*.

The following diagram illustrates Magento's architecture and how the components are integrated:

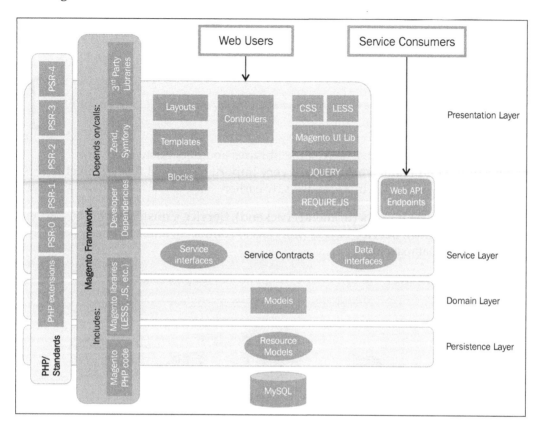

Magento works with **PHP Standards Recommendations (PSR)**. The PSR establishes the following good programming practices:

- **PHP extensions**: This allows Magento to work with some PHP extension solutions that are required by Magento, for example, **PDO** and **Memcache**.

- **PSR-0 — Autoloading Standard**: This enables class autoloading on the PHP code. It's highly recommended to use PSR-4 instead of PSR-0, but the PSR-0 standard illustrates only the Magento architecture standards.

- **PSR-1 — Basic Coding Standard**: These are some good practices to write the PHP code.

- **PSR-2 — Coding Style Guide**: This extends PSR-1, adding the layout code presentation.

- **PSR-3 — Logger Interface**: This exposes eight methods to write logs to the eight RFC 5424 levels (`debug`, `info`, `notice`, `warning`, `error`, `critical`, `alert`, and `emergency`).

- **PSR-4 — Autoloading Standard**: This describes a specification for autoloading classes from file paths.

 To know more about this, access `http://www.php-fig.org/psr/`.

On **Magento Framework**, we have some libraries and dependencies of this architecture. **Zend Framework (ZF)** is a very important layer of this architecture; once Magento was written in ZF; as we saw earlier.

Finally, we have **Web Users** (frontend/backend), **Service Consumers** (API and endpoints), **Service Layers** (interfaces/contracts), and **Models** (resources and database).

On the Web Users layer, we can define Magento's main processes as:

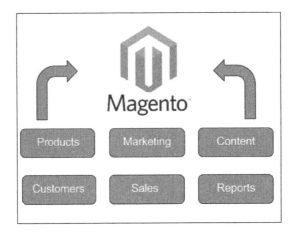

- **Products**: This manages the configuration of products in Magento, such as catalogs, inventory, categories, and attributes
- **Marketing**: This manages promotions, communications, and SEO
- **Content**: This manages the pages content
- **Customers**: This manages and gets information about customers
- **Sales**: This manages cart process, checkout, orders, shipping, and payments
- **Reports**: This generates reports and statics of e-commerce

We will discuss these topics in the coming chapters, but now, I'd like to introduce to you one of the most important processes of any kind of e-commerce: the **Sales** layer or **Magento Order Management**. This is one of the most important things to understand the Magento development core.

An introduction to the Magento order management system

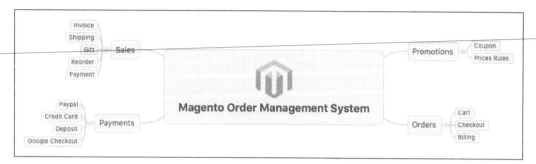

On the e-commerce systems, the sell process is one of the most important features of every online business, providing a good e-commerce life cycle.

Some processes will be triggered when a customer confirms his order. Magento collects all the customer data and processes the request turning it into an order. This book will only cover the basic concepts of this process, but it's very important to understand them to develop consistent Magento extension solutions (we will see about this in *Chapter 6, Write Magento 2.0 Extensions – a Great Place to Go*).

Let's take a look at the Magento sales operations basics.

Sales operations

Let's play with the Magento admin area. In your favorite browser, enter the URL
`http://localhost/packt/admin-packt`. Now, enter with your login credentials
to access the admin area:

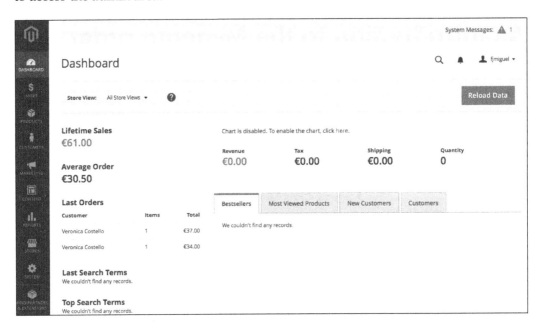

In Magento 2.0, you can manage sales operations by accessing the **Sales** menu in the
admin area. Magento gives you the possibility to configure the following **Sales** options:

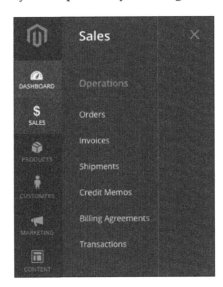

These options give you the power to manage your sales system as you want. Though it's, it's important to explore some Magento tools, extensions, and techniques to take full advantage and make improvements on your sales system to gather techniques to develop your own solution:

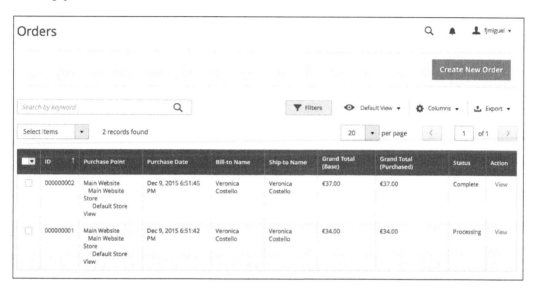

We have many options to make improvements on sales operations. You can configure up-sells and cross-sells features, for example, to give your customer more ways to order on your store. To do so, take advantage of a search engine optimization, work with a multilingual store, a geo-targeting, responsive design, and a simplified checkout process.

A simplified checkout process

In this section, we'll see how to implement a simplified checkout process on our store.

Orders

As a system administrator, you can access the admin area (`http://localhost/mymagento/admin`) to get all the customer order information, generate the product tracking code, invoices, and send a message to your customer. Magento stores all the order data on the **admin area | Sales | Orders**.

As an admin, Magento gives you the option to order products directly for your customer. On Magento, we have a persistent cart, print invoices, credit memo, and transactions.

Payments

You have a few options of payment methods in Magento. Magento has a native support to **Google Checkout** and **PayPal**. They both are payment gateways that provide the entire sell transaction environment to your store.

Basically, you choose your payment method and choose how you will pay for your product: credit card or deposit.

Promotions

With the products prices defined, you can set up promotions in advance. Promotion systems are very useful to establish a solid relationship with the customer.

In Magento, it is possible to define catalog price rules and shopping cart rules. Basically, you can define price behavior according to your promotions and customer defined rules, such as postal code, and certain value of discount.

You can provide coupon codes for your customers to raise Magento sells.

Magento 2.0 command-line configuration

Once you have installed Magento 2.0 CE, you will need to configure some options and manage the system life cycle according to your specific needs. You can start your Magento configuration and administration using the **command-line utility**.

Let's see how this feature works.

The command-line utility

Magento 2.0 has a command-line utility to help developers manage installation and configuration tasks. The new command-line interface can do the following:

- Install Magento
- Manage the cache
- Manage indexers
- Configure and run cron
- Compile code
- Set the Magento mode
- Set the URN highlighter

- Create dependency reports
- Translate dictionaries and language packages
- Deploy static view files
- Create symlinks to LESS files
- Run unit tests
- Convert layout into XML files
- Generate data for performance testing
- Create CSS from LESS (CSS real-time compilation)

To work with this tool, you will need to open a terminal (Linux, OS X) or command prompt (Windows) and access the `<your Magento install dir>/bin` directory. Then, enter with the `php magento` command to see all the available commands of the command-line utility:

```
[FernandoMiguel:bin fjmiguel$ cd /Applications/XAMPP/htdocs/packt/bin/
[FernandoMiguel:bin fjmiguel$ php magento --list
Magento CLI version 2.0.0

Usage:
 command [options] [arguments]

Options:
 --help (-h)              Display this help message
 --quiet (-q)             Do not output any message
 --verbose (-v|vv|vvv)    Increase the verbosity of messages: 1 for normal output,
 --version (-V)           Display this application version
 --ansi                   Force ANSI output
 --no-ansi                Disable ANSI output
 --no-interaction (-n)    Do not ask any interactive question

Available commands:
 help                     Displays help for a command
 list                     Lists commands
admin
 admin:user:create        Creates an administrator
 admin:user:unlock        Unlock Admin Account
```

 Remember to configure the PHP path to the system environment variable to execute the command. For further information, access `http://php.net/manual/en/faq.installation.php`.

Let's play a little bit with the utility by disabling your Magento system cache:

- Run the `php magento cache:status` command. The cache will probably be enabled.

- Run the `php magento cache:disable` command to disable any cache system.

```
[FernandoMiguel:bin fjmiguel$ php magento cache:status
Current status:
                        config: 1
                        layout: 1
                    block_html: 1
                   collections: 1
                    reflection: 1
                        db_ddl: 1
                           eav: 1
            config_integration: 1
        config_integration_api: 1
                     full_page: 1
                     translate: 1
             config_webservice: 1
[FernandoMiguel:bin fjmiguel$ php magento cache:disable
Changed cache status:
                        config: 1 -> 0
                        layout: 1 -> 0
                    block_html: 1 -> 0
                   collections: 1 -> 0
                    reflection: 1 -> 0
                        db_ddl: 1 -> 0
                           eav: 1 -> 0
            config_integration: 1 -> 0
        config_integration_api: 1 -> 0
                     full_page: 1 -> 0
                     translate: 1 -> 0
             config_webservice: 1 -> 0
FernandoMiguel:bin fjmiguel$
```

 To know more about cache management in command-utility tools, access http://goo.gl/c5ivCY.http://goo.gl/c5ivCY.

Now let's try to manage Magento indexing. Magento indexing transforms the data to improve the performance of your system by executing the following commands. Indexing technique optimizes the price calculations process, for example, and it has an important role to play in the Magento performance:

- Run the php magento indexer:info command to view the lists of indexers
- Run the php magento indexer:status command to view the real-time status
- Run the php magento indexer:reindex command to rebuild the indexation

```
[FernandoMiguel:bin fjmiguel$ php magento indexer:info
customer_grid                          Customer Grid
catalog_category_product               Category Products
catalog_product_category               Product Categories
catalog_product_price                  Product Price
catalog_product_attribute              Product EAV
cataloginventory_stock                 Stock
catalogsearch_fulltext                 Catalog Search
catalogrule_rule                       Catalog Rule Product
catalogrule_product                    Catalog Product Rule
[FernandoMiguel:bin fjmiguel$ php magento indexer:status
Customer Grid:                                      Ready
Category Products:                                  Reindex required
Product Categories:                                 Reindex required
Product Price:                                      Ready
Product EAV:                                        Ready
Stock:                                              Ready
Catalog Search:                                     Ready
Catalog Rule Product:                               Reindex required
Catalog Product Rule:                               Ready
[FernandoMiguel:bin fjmiguel$ php magento indexer:reindex
Customer Grid index has been rebuilt successfully in 00:00:04
Category Products index has been rebuilt successfully in 00:00:01
Product Categories index has been rebuilt successfully in 00:00:00
Product Price index has been rebuilt successfully in 00:00:04
Product EAV index has been rebuilt successfully in 00:00:03
Stock index has been rebuilt successfully in 00:00:01
Catalog Search index has been rebuilt successfully in 00:00:04
Catalog Rule Product index has been rebuilt successfully in 00:00:05
Catalog Product Rule index has been rebuilt successfully in 00:00:03
```

Magento indexing was successfully rebuilt, thanks to the command-line utility actions!

You can build **cron** jobs in a remote server to automate some Magento actions. For example, create an automation routine to re-index Magento periodically.

I strongly advise you to play more with the command-line utility. You can consult the online documentation available at http://goo.gl/iVnQSn.

Summary

We started this chapter to get the real bases of Magento power. It's important to get solid concepts, before you eagerly jump and begin developing Magento solutions. Take a moment to understand the scope of your project. This will make Magento development a much more rewarding experience.

Magento has a solid structure to develop your own solutions. You can automate some tasks using the Magento command-line utility and optimize Magento resources to get better results.

In the next chapter, we will work with Magento search engine optimization.

3
Working with Search Engine Optimization

Search Engine Optimization (SEO) is a technique to build your site following good practices established by W3C Consortium and search engines, such as Google, to increase your site's visitation and ranking. On Magento, we need to configure the system properly to take advantage of this feature. Nowadays, SEO is a prerequisite on every website on the Internet.

Magento has a great variety of tools to configure the store of SEO and allows SEO adjustment for products, categories and CMS page titles, metainformation, and headings.

SEO application is a constant job; it never ends. Basically, you need to know how Magento SEO works and what options you have to optimize its working. Magento is a search engine-friendly e-commerce platform, and you will discover its main concepts in this chapter.

In this book, you will learn some good techniques and apply them by configuring the default installation.

The following topics will be covered in this chapter:

- Magento SEO management
- SEO catalog configuration
- XML sitemap manager
- Google Analytics tracking code
- Optimizing Magento pages, products, and categories

Magento SEO management

SEO is the technique of developing a site according to the high standards defined by the World Wide Web Consortium and search engine companies, such as Google, in order to provide good content visualization to the users and rank the site in organic searches.

Magento provides the user with some significant tools for SEO. Let's take a look at some of these techniques and tools.

Store configuration

By default, Magento's basic installation has the title `Magento Commerce` on the header settings. It is very important to choose a strong main title to get the right amount of traffic on your site. For example, if you are working on the SEO of a sports store, you can set the main title as **My Sports Store** to increase the traffic through the title. When people search for something, they always notice the earlier words first.

HTML Head		
Favicon Icon	Choose File no file selected Allowed file types: ICO, PNG, GIF, JPG, JPEG, APNG, SVG. Not all browsers support all these formats!	[STORE VIEW]
Default Title	Magento Commerce	[STORE VIEW]
Title Prefix		[STORE VIEW]
Title Suffix		[STORE VIEW]
Default Description	Default Description	[STORE VIEW]
Default Keywords	Magento, Varien, E-commerce	[STORE VIEW]
Miscellaneous Scripts	`<link rel="stylesheet" type="text/css" media="all" href=" {{MEDIA_URL}}styles.css" />` This will be included before head closing tag in page HTML.	[STORE VIEW]
Display Demo Store Notice	No	[STORE VIEW]

To adjust your store settings, you need to navigate to **Stores | Configuration | Design | HTML Head** in the Magento admin area (`http://localhost/packt/ admin-packt`).

Choose a good descriptive title for your Magento commerce. It is possible and recommended to name all your page titles, including categories and products, by entering the site title in the **Title Suffix** field. To give density to the content for SEO engines by configuring the SEO on CMS pages and products, keep **Default Description** and **Default Keywords** empty.

For a local and nonproduction environment, prevent the indexing of the site by setting **Default Robots** to `NOINDEX, NOFOLLOW`. Otherwise, it is recommended to set it to `INDEX, FOLLOW`.

By working on this configuration, you will find that the main SEO parameters of the `<head>` tag are automatically fulfilled to be run on Magento commerce.

SEO and searching

Magento has a specific SEO configuration panel for multiple sections. To access the main Magento SEO configuration, enter in the Magento admin area (`http:// localhost/packt/admin-packt`), and you will find the panel by clicking on the menu at **Marketing | SEO & Search**:

Magento 2.0 changed some functionality in comparison with its previous version. For example, in the **URL Rewrites** menu, you can manage and define all the URL addresses of Magento in order to increase the SEO's friendly URLs.

Here, you can simply choose **Request Path** to edit and enter a description for each of them, as shown in the following screenshot:

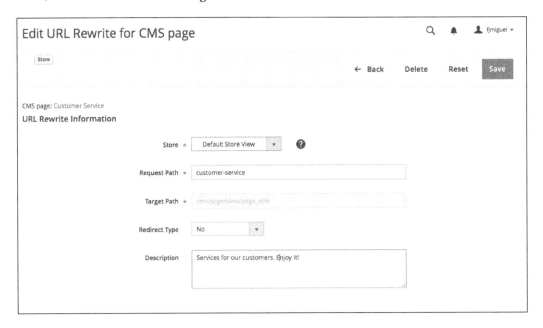

In **Search Terms**, you can define and redirect the URL according to the search made by the user by adding a new search term:

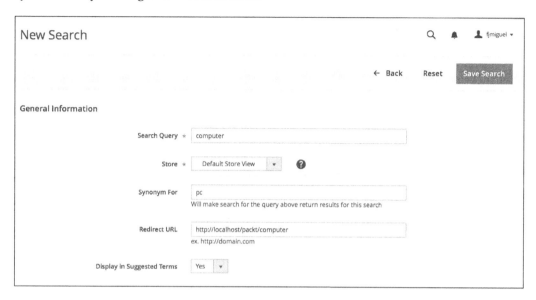

Finally, in the **New Site Map** section, you can generate **Sitemap** of your Magento installation as shown in the following screenshot:

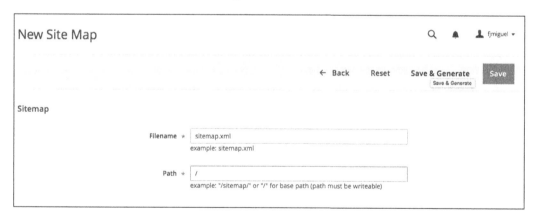

SEO catalog configuration

Magento has a special panel to take care of the catalog categories of SEO. To access this panel, navigate to **Stores | Configuration | Catalog | Search Engine Optimization**, as follows:

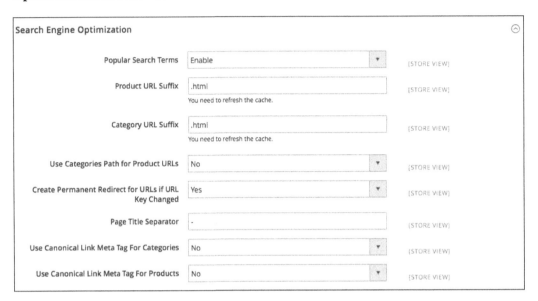

This panel has the following options:

- **Popular Search Terms**: This allows pages to display your most popular search phrases. Set this to **Yes**.

- **Product URL Suffix**: This is the suffix that is added to the end of your product URLs.

- **Category URL Suffix**: This is the suffix that is added to the end of your category URLs.

- **Use Categories Path for Product URLs**: This includes the category URL in your URL string.

- **Create Permanent Redirect for URLs if URL Key Changed**: This automatically creates a redirect via the URL Rewrites' module in Magento if the URL key is changed in any page on your website.

- **Page Title Separator**: This separates the page titles on the frontend of your store.

- **Use Canonical Link Meta Tag For Categories**: This displays the main version of the category page. This is picked up by search engines to avoid duplicate content.

- **Use Canonical Link Meta Tag For Products**: This has the same functionality as the previous item, but it works on the products layer.

Source: http://slpxya.appspot.com/moz.com/ugc/
setting-up-magento-for-the-search-engines.

With these options, you can choose the best strategy for SEO on catalog's default options. Magenta gives the administrator the opportunity to tune these options on catalog pages. We will work this out later in this chapter.

XML sitemap manager

Magento automatically generates an XML sitemap for your store and also keeps it up to date. In order to enable this, navigate to **Stores** | **Configuration** | **Catalog** | **XML Sitemap**. Magento has the following options for this section:

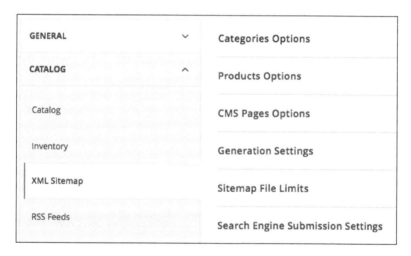

Basically, with these options, it is possible to choose the frequency and priority of updates. You may set additional options, such as **Start Time** and **Error Notifications**, only in the **GENERAL** settings tab. It's important to configure the cron job functionality in your web server to enable this feature.

Google Analytics tracking code

Google Analytics helps track all the statistics for your site. To add Google Analytics on Magento, generate a tracking code on your Google Analytics account (`http://analytics.google.com`) first of all. After this, navigate to **System** | **Configuration** | **Google API**.

This option works only on hosted Magento sites (that is, the remote server). Take note of this for when you work on a remote production Magento site. For the purposes of this book, it isn't necessary, but you need to keep this option in mind when you start to work on remote projects.

Optimizing Magento pages

Once you make Magento SEO system configurations, it's time to set specific options directly on Magento pages. This Magento SEO flow gives the user the flexibility to focus on content and page ranking.

CMS pages

The Magento **Content Management System (CMS)** manager is a very simple but powerful tool that provides us with control over each aspect of the Magento page. To access Magento CMS pages configuration in the admin area, go to **Content** | **Pages**, as shown in the following screenshot:

Magento's default installation provides some demo content to test CMS pages. Check the **Home Page** content by selecting the **Edit** option.

For the purpose of SEO, Magento's CMS page administration has two main SEO side menus: **Page Information** and **Meta Data**.

In **Page Information**, you can set the following options:

- **Page Title**: This should correspond to the main title of the page
- **URL Key**: This is very important to set a great **Search Engine Friendly (SEF)** URL identifier to increase SEO ranking
- **Store View**: Here, you can choose the views on the page
- **Status**: This has simple **Enabled** and **Disabled** options.

In **Meta Data**, you can set the following options:

- **Keywords**: Here, enter the keywords that correspond to your site's scope.
- **Description**: Make sure to use this field the right way. A good description means a good chance of increasing access and sales.

The content of your page must be aligned with the metadata for a good SEO implementation.

Product pages

This is the most important layer in a Magento store. Besides providing a lot of options to configure the product to be sold, this also makes it possible to tune the SEO configuration to increase sales through the search engine page ranking system. In order to access **Product** options, navigate to **Products | Catalog**, as shown in the following screenshot:

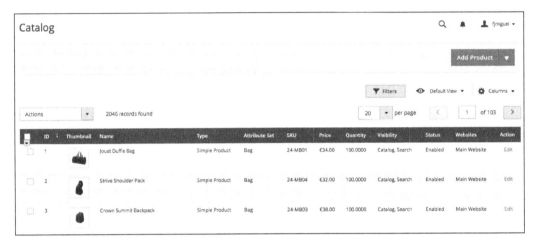

Click on the first product of the list to take a look at the SEO options. For the purpose of SEO, **Product Details** has the following options:

- **Name**: You need to make this descriptive; think about what people might search for

- **Description**: Here, you must detail the product as much as possible to make your content unique and helpful to users

- **Categories**: This is the category of the product.

Search Engine Optimization has the following options:

- **URL Key**: This is the URL that the product will be visible on. If the product has a version number or some specific detail, try to put this on the URL.

- **Meta Information**: Choose the best **Meta Title**, **Meta Keywords**, and **Meta Description** input for your product.

Every single product gives the administrator these options to tune SEO on a Magento website.

Category pages

Magento category pages have great SEO options. As you can note, all the content pages on Magento give us administration options to manage SEO. Every aspect on Magento configuration is integrated to provide the user with the best experience.

To access the **Categories** configuration, navigate to **Products | Categories** on the admin dashboard, as shown in the following screenshot:

This will provide an option to create a new category, and in the side menu, it is possible to check all the categories registered on Magento. For the purpose of SEO, Magento has the following options in this section:

- **Name**: This is the category name.
- **Description**: This is the description of the category. Focus on using keywords strategically for SEO.
- **Page Title**: This refers to the metatitle. Enter your keyword with a few words to describe the page.
- **Meta Keywords**: Here, enter the keywords separated by commas.
- **Meta Description**: This is a very important option, so make sure that your description covers the products that you're selling and reinforces your brand.

Make sure to follow a pattern in your content referring to SEO.

Summary

Magento SEO is a powerful tool to increase sales. As a developer, it is very important to keep these options and techniques in mind to create mechanisms that would get better results for Magento users through new extensions and customizations.

In this chapter, we discussed the following:

- Magento SEO management
- SEO catalog configuration
- XML sitemap manager
- Google Analytics tracking code
- Optimizing Magento pages, products, and categories

In the next chapter, we will cover Magento theme development and customization. We have a lot of work coming up!

4
Magento 2.0 Theme Development – the Developers' Holy Grail

Magento 2.0 has a complex control of its themes. It works with multiple directories to generate the final result for the user on its frontend.

In this chapter we will consolidate the basic concepts that you need to create your very first example of Magento theme and activate it.

At the end of this chapter, you will be able to create the basic structure of your own theme. The following topics are covered in this chapter:

- The basic concepts of Magento themes
- Magento 2.0 theme structure
- The Magento Luma theme
- Magento theme inheritance
- CMS blocks and pages
- Custom variables
- Creating a basic Magento 2.0 theme

The basic concepts of Magento themes

According to the official documentation available at `http://goo.gl/D4oxO1`, a **Magento theme** is a component that provides the visual design for an entire application area using a combination of custom templates, layouts, styles, or images. Themes are implemented by different vendors (frontend developers) and intended to be distributed as additional packages for Magento systems similar to other components.

Magento has its own particularities because it is based on Zend Framework and consequently adopts the MVC architecture as a software design pattern. When the Magento theme process flow becomes a subject, you have some concerns to worry about when you plan to create your own theme. Let's focus on these concepts to create our own theme by the end of this chapter.

Magento 2.0 theme structure

Magento 2.0 has a new approach toward managing its themes. Generally, the Magento 2.0 themes are located in the `app/design/frontend/<Vendor>/` directory. This location differs according to the built-in themes, such as the **Luma** theme, which is located in `vendor/magento/theme-frontend-luma`.

The different themes are stored in separate directories, as in the following screenshot:

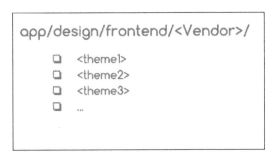

Each vendor can have one or more themes attached to it. So, you can develop different themes inside the same vendor.

The theme structure of Magento 2.0 is illustrated as follows:

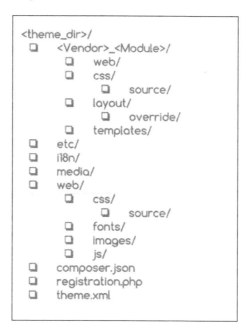

How the Magento theme structure works is quite simple to understand: each `<Vendor>_<Module>` directory corresponds to a specific module or functionality of your theme. For example, `Magento_Customer` has specific `.css` and `.html` files to handle the `Customer` module of the `Magento` vendor. Magento handles a significant number of modules. So, I strongly suggest that you navigate to the `vendor/magento/theme-frontend-luma` folder to take a look at the available modules for the default theme.

In the Magento 2.0 structure, we have three main files that manage the theme behavior, which are as follows:

- `composer.json`: This file describes the dependencies and meta information
- `registration.php`: This file registers your theme in the system
- `theme.xml`: This file declares the theme in system and is used by the Magento system to recognize the theme

All the theme files inside the structure explained previously can be divided into **static view files** and **dynamic view files**. The static view files have no processing by the server (images, fonts, and `.js` files), and the dynamic view files are processed by the server before delivering the content to the user (template and layout files).

Static files are generally published in the following folders:

- `/pub/static/frontend/<Vendor>/<theme>/<language>`
- `<theme_dir>/media/`
- `<theme_dir>/web`

 For further information, please access the official Magento theme structure documentation at `http://goo.gl/ov3IUJ`.

The Magento Luma theme

The Magento CE 2.0 version comes with a new theme named Luma that implements **Responsive Web Design (RWD)** practices.

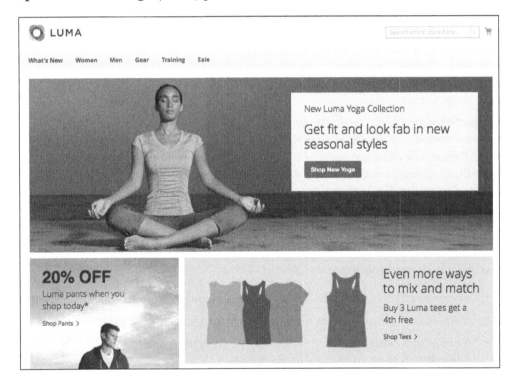

The Luma theme style is based on the Magento **user interface** (UI) library and uses CSS3 media queries to work with screen width, adapting the layout according to device access.

The Magento UI is a great toolbox for theme development in Magento 2.0 and provides the following components to customize and reuse user interface elements:

- The actions toolbar
- Breadcrumbs
- Buttons
- Drop-down menus
- Forms
- Icons
- Layout
- Loaders
- Messages
- Pagination
- Popups
- Ratings
- Sections
- Tabs and accordions
- Tables
- Tooltips
- Typography
- A list of theme variables

The Luma theme uses some of the **blank** theme features to be functional. The Magento 2.0 blank theme, available in the `vendor/magento/theme-frontend-blank` folder, is the basic Magento theme and is declared as the **parent theme** of Luma. How is this possible? Logically, Magento has distinct folders for every theme, but Magento is too smart to reuse code; it takes advantage of **theme inheritance**. Let's take a look at how this works.

Magento theme inheritance

The frontend of Magento allows designers to create new themes based on the basic blank theme, reusing the main code without changing its structure. The fallback system is a theme's inheritance mechanism and allows developers to create only the files that are necessary for customization.

The Luma theme, for example, uses the fallback system by inheriting the blank theme basic structure. The Luma theme parent is declared in its `theme.xml` file as follows:

```
<theme xmlns:xsi="http://www.w3.org/2001/XMLSchema-instance" xsi:noNam
espaceSchemaLocation="urn:magento:framework:Config/etc/theme.xsd">
    <title>Magento Luma</title>
    <parent>Magento/blank</parent>
    <media>
        <preview_image>media/preview.jpg</preview_image>
    </media>
</theme>
```

Inheritance works similar to an override system. You can create new themes using the existent ones (parents) and by replacing (that is, overriding) an existing file with the same name but in your specific theme folder (child).

For example, if you create a new theme in the `app/design/frontend/<Vendor>/<theme>/` folder and declare `Magento/blank` as a parent theme, the `theme.xml` file and `registration.php`, you have the entire blank theme structure ready to work in your new theme, including RWD layouts and styles.

Let's say that you have a specific `.css` file available in the `<theme_dir>/web/css` folder. If you delete this file, the fallback system will search the file in the `<parent_theme_dir>/web/css` folder, as shown in the following figure:

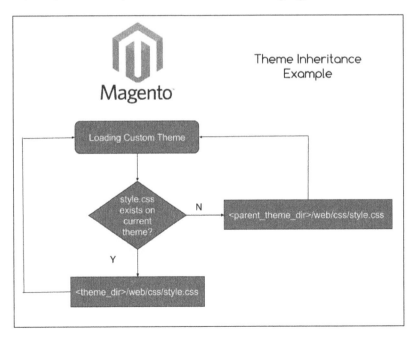

CMS blocks and pages

Magento has a flexible theme system. Beyond Magento code customization, the admin can create blocks and content on the Magento admin panel, such as **Home Page**, **About us**, or any static page that you want to create. CMS pages and blocks on Magento give you the power to embed HTML code in your page.

You can create or edit pages and blocks by accessing the Admin area (`http://localhost/packt/admin_packt`) by navigating to **Content | Pages**.

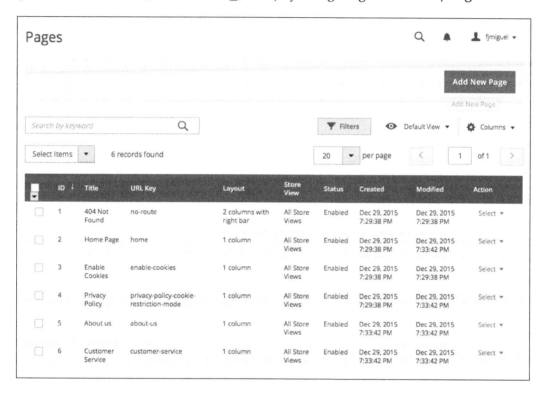

Custom variables

Custom variables are pieces of HTML code that contain specific values as programming variables. By creating a custom variable, you can apply it to multiple areas on your site. An example of the custom variable structure is shown here:

```
{{config path="web/unsecure/base_url"}}
```

This variable shows the URL of the store.

Now, let's create a custom variable to see how it works. Perform the following steps:

1. Open your favorite browser and access the admin area through `http://localhost/packt/admin_packt`.

2. Navigate to **System | Custom Variables**

3. Then, click on the **Add New Variable** button.

4. In the **Variable Code** field, enter the variable in lowercase with no spaces—for example, `dev_name`.

5. Enter the variable name, which explains the variable purpose.

6. Enter the HTML and plain text values of the custom variable in the **Variable HTML Value** and **Variable Plain Value** fields and save it.

Now, we have a custom variable that stores the developer's name. Let's use this variable inside the CMS **About Us** page via the following steps:

1. In the **Admin** area, navigate to **Content | Pages**.

2. Click to edit the **About Us** item.

3. Then, click on the **Content** side menu.

4. Click on the **Show / Hide Editor** button to hide the HTML editor.

5. Put the following code at the end of the content:

   ```
   {{CustomVar code="dev_name"}}
   ```

6. Finally, save the content.

Content

Content Heading   About us

Show / Hide Editor

```
<div class="about-info cms-content">
<p class="cms-content-important">With more than 230 stores spanning 43 states and
growing, Luma is a nationally recognized active wear manufacturer and retailer.
We&rsquo;re passionate about active lifestyles &ndash; and it goes way beyond apparel.
</p>
<p>At Luma, wellness is a way of life. We don&rsquo;t believe age, gender or past actions
define you, only your ambition and desire for wholeness... today.</p>
<p>We differentiate ourselves through a combination of unique designs and styles merged
with unequaled standards of quality and authenticity. Our founders have deep roots in yoga
and health communities and our selections serve amateur practitioners and professional
athletes alike.</p>
<ul style="list-style: none; margin-top: 20px; padding: 0;">
<li><a href="{{store url="contact"}}">Contact Luma</a></li>
<li><a href="{{store url="customer-service"}}">Customer Service</a></li>
<li><a href="{{store url="privacy-policy"}}">Luma Privacy Policy</a></li>
<li><a href="{{store url=""}}">Shop Luma</a></li>
</ul>
<p>Developer: {{CustomVar code="dev_name"}} </p>
</div>
```

Let's take a look at the result in the following screenshot:

Creating a basic Magento 2.0 theme

After understanding the basic Magento 2.0 theme structure, you have the right credentials to go to the next level: creating your own theme. In this chapter, we will develop a simple theme and activate it on the **Magento Admin** panel. The basic idea is to give you the right directions to Magento theme development and provide you with the tools to let your imagination fly around the creation of various Magento themes!

Before starting the creation, let's disable Magento **cache management**. It is important when you work with Magento development to get updates in real time. You learned about cache management in *Chapter 2, Magento 2.0 Features*:

1. Open the terminal (Linux, OS X) or command prompt (Windows) and access the `<your Magento install dir>/bin` directory.

2. Then, run the `php magento cache:disable` command to disable all the cache systems.

```
[MacBook-Pro:bin fjmiguel$ php magento cache:disable
Changed cache status:
                         config: 1 -> 0
                         layout: 1 -> 0
                     block_html: 1 -> 0
                    collections: 1 -> 0
                     reflection: 1 -> 0
                         db_ddl: 1 -> 0
                            eav: 1 -> 0
             config_integration: 1 -> 0
         config_integration_api: 1 -> 0
                      full_page: 1 -> 0
                      translate: 1 -> 0
              config_webservice: 1 -> 0
MacBook-Pro:bin fjmiguel$ █
```

Creating and declaring a theme

To create a basic theme structure, follow these steps:

1. Create a new vendor directory named `Packt` at the following path:

   `<Magento root directory>/app/design/frontend/`**`Packt`**

2. Under the `Packt` directory, create the theme directory named `basic` by executing the following:

   `<Magento root directory>/app/design/frontend/`**`Packt/basic`**

The next step is to declare the theme information for Magento to recognize it as a new theme. Perform the following:

1. Open your preferred code editor (**Sublime Text2**, **TextMate**, **Atom.io**).

2. Create a new file named `theme.xml` under your theme directory (`app/design/frontend/Packt/basic/theme.xml`).

3. Use the following code in the `theme.xml` file and save the file:

```
<theme xmlns:xsi="http://www.w3.org/2001/XMLSchema-instance" xsi:n
oNamespaceSchemaLocation="urn:magento:framework:Config/etc/theme.
xsd">
    <title>Basic theme</title>
    <parent>Magento/blank</parent>
    <!-- <media>
        <preview_image>media/preview.jpg</preview_image>
    </media>-->
</theme>
```

This is a basic declaration for the Magento system to recognize our theme as an official theme. This code configures the theme name, parent, and preview image. The preview image is a preview for basic visualization purposes. We don't have a preview image right now, which is the why the code is commented; avoid unnecessary errors.

Once we have the basic configurations, we need to register the theme in the Magento system:

1. Open your preferred code editor (**Sublime Text2**, **TextMate**, or **Atom.io**).

2. Create new file named `registration.php` under your theme directory (`app/design/frontend/Packt/basic/registration.php`).

3. Use the following code in registration.php and save the file:

```php
<?php
/**
 * Copyright © 2016 Magento. All rights reserved.
 * See COPYING.txt for license details.
 */
\Magento\Framework\Component\ComponentRegistrar::register(
    \Magento\Framework\Component\ComponentRegistrar::THEME,
    'frontend/Packt/basic',
    __DIR__
);
```

This code simply registers our theme in the Magento system by passing a parameter of your new theme's structure directory.

Simple product image configuration

In your theme, you can configure the image properties of the products in the Magento Catalog module by creating the `view.xml` file. You can control this specific configuration using the `id` attribute of every product's HTML5 element:

1. Open your preferred code editor (Sublime Text2, TextMate, or Atom.io).

2. Create a new directory named `etc` under your theme directory (`app/design/frontend/Packt/basic/etc`).

3. Create a new file named `view.xml` under your `etc` directory (`app/design/frontend/Packt/basic/etc/view.xml`).

4. Then, use the following code in `view.xml` and save the file:

```xml
<image id="category_page_grid" type="small_image">
        <width>250</width>
```

```
        <height>250</height>
    </image>
```

In the `view.xml` file, we declared the values of the width and height of the product image. The `id` and `type` attributes specified the kind of image that this rule will be applied to.

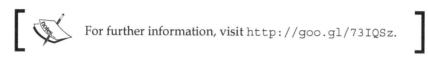 For further information, visit `http://goo.gl/73IQSz`.

Creating static files' directories

The static files (images, `.js` files, `.css` files, and fonts) will be stored in the `web` directory. Inside the `web` directory, we will organize our static files according to its scope. Create a new directory named `web` under your `directory app/design/frontend/Packt/basic/web` theme and create the following directory structure:

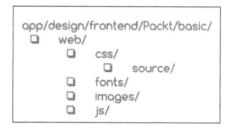

With this simple structure, you can manage all the static files of your custom theme.

Creating a theme logo

By default in Magento 2.0, the theme logo is always recognized by the system by the name `logo.svg`. Magento 2.0 also recognizes the logo's default directory as `<theme_dir>/web/images/logo.svg`. So, if you have a `logo.svg` file, you can simply put the file in the right directory.

However, if you want to work with a different logo's name with a different format, you have to declare it in the Magento system. We will make a declaration with this new logo in the `Magento_Theme` directory because the new logo is a customization of the `Magento_Theme` module. We will override this module by taking advantage of the fallback system. As you may note, Magento has a specific pattern of declaring elements. This is the way in which Magento organizes its life cycle.

Let's declare a new theme logo by performing the following steps:

1. Choose one logo for the example and save the file as `logo.png` in the `app/design/frontend/Packt/basic/Magento_Theme/web/images` directory.

2. Open your preferred code editor (Sublime Text2, TextMate, or Atom.io).

3. Create new file named `default.xml` under your `layout` directory (`app/design/frontend/Packt/basic/Magento_Theme/layout`).

4. Use the following code in `default.xml` and save the file:

```
<page xmlns:xsi="http://www.w3.org/2001/XMLSchema-instance" xsi:n
oNamespaceSchemaLocation="urn:magento:framework:View/Layout/etc/
page_configuration.xsd">
    <body>
        <referenceBlock name="logo">
            <arguments>
                <argument name="logo_file" xsi:type="string">
Magento_Theme/images/logo.png
</argument>
                <argument name="logo_img_width" xsi:type="number">
your_logo_width
</argument>
<argument name="logo_img_height" xsi:type="number">
your_logo_height
</argument>
            </arguments>
        </referenceBlock>
    </body>
</page>
```

This declaration has three different arguments to manage three attributes of your new logo: filename, width, and height. Don't forget to replace the `your_logo_width` and `your_logo_height` attributes with the correct size of the logo that you choose.

The `logo_file` argument seems to be wrong because we created our image in the `Magento_Theme/web/images` directory; however, thank God this is not true. I'll explain: when we activate the new theme, Magento processes the static files and copies them to the `pub/static` directory. This occurs because static files can be cached by Magento, and the correct directory for this is `pub`. So, we need to create the `web` directory for Magento to recognize the files as static files.

The final theme directory structure is illustrated as follows:

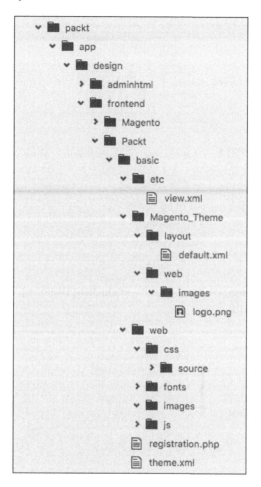

Applying the theme

Once we have the theme ready to launch, we need to activate it in the Magento admin dashboard:

1. First, access the Magento admin area URL (`http://localhost/packt/admin_packt`) in your favorite browser.

2. Navigate to **Stores** | **Configuration** | **Design**.

3. Then, select the **Basic theme** option as your **Design Theme** value and save the configuration.

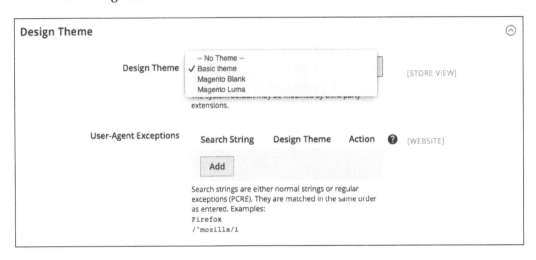

Navigate to the home page of your site by accessing the `http://localhost/packt` URL to see the final result:

Summary

Now, you have all the basic concepts to create a custom theme for Magento and all the information to think in terms of the Magento structure when an idea for your new design comes to mind.

In this chapter, you learned the basic concepts of Magento 2.0 themes, how theme inheritance (that is, the fallback system) works, and which directories Magento uses to create its themes according to the admin area configurations. Finally, you created your own basic theme with these examples.

However, what about creating a quality theme? Is it possible with the knowledge acquired in this chapter? Of course! We will go to the next level in the next chapter and create a responsive theme by example.

5
Creating a Responsive Magento 2.0 Theme

In the previous chapter, you learned the fundamentals of creating a custom Magento 2.0 theme, and we created the basic structure by example. In this chapter, we will create our own theme project called the **CompStore** theme.

The following topics will be covered in this chapter:

- Developing the CompStore theme
- Introduction to Composer Dependency Manager
- CSS preprocessing with LESS
- Creating new content for the CompStore theme
- Developing a custom CompStore theme using CSS
- Creating a custom template

The CompStore theme

The CompStore theme project is the new Magento 2.0 theme that you will develop for a hypothetical computer store client or for a theme marketplace such as `http://themeforest.net/`. I strongly suggest you to take a look at the **Become an author** page at `http://themeforest.net/become_an_author` in order to explore the options to monetize your Magento theme development expertise. Logically, you have to work harder before publishing and selling your own theme solution, but it will be worth it!

Magento 2.0 themes and modules work with the **Composer** (`https://getcomposer.org/`) dependency manager for PHP to generate a reliable deployment of Magento components. This is a great evolution in the Magento universe because this management can provide a powerful environment for the deployment of modules and themes. So, we will create a `composer` file for our new theme solution.

Before we start the theme development, let's take a look at Composer.

Composer – the PHP dependency manager

Inspired by **npm** (`https://www.npmjs.com/`) and **bundler** (`http://bundler.io/`), Composer (`https://getcomposer.org/`) manages the dependencies of your project and installs packages in predetermined directories (for example, `vendor`) using the `composer.json` file in the Magento module or theme. This kind of management is very useful once each library has your specific dependency. Composer doesn't let you waste your time by connecting the dependencies to every deployment that you want to do.

In the next chapters, we will use Composer to install components on Magento. However, first, we will start the development of our theme; it is necessary to declare our composer.json file. For now, let's install Composer on the operating system.

Installing Composer on Unix-like operating systems

To install Composer on Unix-like systems (such as Unix, Linux, and OS X), you simply need to run these two commands in the terminal:

```
$ curl -s https://getcomposer.org/installer | php
$ sudo mv composer.phar /usr/local/bin/composer
```

The first command downloads the composer.phar installation file. The second command moves the file to the bin directory to install Composer globally on your computer.

Run the following command to check whether Composer was successfully installed:

```
$ composer
```

The $ composer command lists all the available Composer commands and their descriptions:

```
MacBook-Pro:/ fjmiguel$ composer


   _____
  / ____/___  ____ ___  ____  ____  _____  _____
 / /   / __ \/ __ `__ \/ __ \/ __ \/ ___/ _ \/ ___/
/ /___/ /_/ / / / / / / /_/ / /_/ (__  )  __/ /
\____/\____/_/ /_/ /_/ .___/\____/____/\___/_/
                    /_/
Composer version 1.0-dev (72cd6afdfce16f36a9fd786bc1b2f32b851e764f) 2

Usage:
  command [options] [arguments]

Options:
  -h, --help                     Display this help message
  -q, --quiet                    Do not output any message
  -V, --version                  Display this application version
      --ansi                     Force ANSI output
      --no-ansi                  Disable ANSI output
  -n, --no-interaction           Do not ask any interactive question
      --profile                  Display timing and memory usage info
  -d, --working-dir=WORKING-DIR  If specified, use the given director
  -v|vv|vvv, --verbose           Increase the verbosity of messages:
3 for debug
```

Installing Composer on Windows

To install Composer on Windows, you simply have to download and execute `Composer-Setup.exe`, which is available on `https://getcomposer.org/Composer-Setup.exe`.

This executable file will install the latest Composer version and set up your path to use the `composer` command in the command prompt window. Open the command prompt window and run `command composer` to get the list of available commands of Composer.

Building the CompStore theme

As you noted in the previous chapter, Magento can store different themes inside the same vendor scope. The proposal project called CompStore will be a template of the Packt vendor. This is the same vendor created in the previous chapter.

First of all, it is important to build the theme directory in the `Packt` vendor directory (`<Magento root directory>/app/design/frontend/Packt/compstore`). Create this folder as the following image suggests:

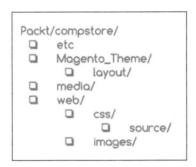

```
Packt/compstore/
    ❏   etc
    ❏   Magento_Theme/
            ❏   layout/
    ❏   media/
    ❏   web/
            ❏   css/
                    ❏   source/
            ❏   images/
```

The `etc` directory usually handles the XML configuration of some components. The `Magento_Theme` directory will override the native `Magento_Theme` module by adding new functionalities. The `media` directory will store the preview image of the CompStore theme. Meanwhile, the `web` directory would have store CSS and image files by now.

The Compstore theme will have Luma as the parent theme. This example shows you the power of the abstraction used in Magento theme projects. Create the `theme.xml` file in the `Packt/compstore` directory with the following code:

```
<theme xmlns:xsi="http://www.w3.org/2001/XMLSchema-instance" xsi:noNam
espaceSchemaLocation="urn:magento:framework:Config/etc/theme.xsd">
    <title>CompStore Electronics</title>
```

```
<parent>Magento/luma</parent>
<media>
    <preview_image>media/preview.jpg</preview_image>
</media>
</theme>
```

The `theme.xml` file declares the title and parent of the CompStore theme. Create a simple `preview.jpg` image with a size of 800 x 800 and save it in the `Packt/compstore/media` directory. For example, the Magento logo is centered at the image size of 800 x 800.

This image shows the preview of the new theme, but as you don't have a preview yet, you can create a placeholder for now.

The next step is creating the `registration.php` file in the `Packt/compstore` directory with the following code:

```
<?php

\Magento\Framework\Component\ComponentRegistrar::register(
    \Magento\Framework\Component\ComponentRegistrar::THEME,
    'frontend/Packt/compstore',
    __DIR__
);
```

In the `registration.php` file, the CompStore theme of the `Packt` vendor registers the new theme of the Magento system.

The `theme.xml` and `registration.php` files were created earlier. By now, I think you are very comfortable with the structure of these files because you worked with them in the basic theme and now in the CompStore theme. This point forward, you will be introduced to some new concepts of theme development in Magento 2.0, starting with the creation of the `composer.json` file. Create the `composer.json` file in the `Packt/compstore` directory with the following code:

```
{
    "name": "packt/compstore",
    "description": "CompStore electronics theme",
    "require": {
        "php": "~5.5.0|~5.6.0|~7.0.0",
        "magento/theme-frontend-luma": "~100.0",
        "magento/framework": "~100.0"
    },
    "type": "magento2-theme",
    "version": "1.0.0",
    "license": [
```

```
        "OSL-3.0",
        "AFL-3.0"
    ],
    "autoload": {
        "files": [ "registration.php" ]
    }
}
```

This file has the `.json` (`http://www.json.org/`) format and handles important information of the project and its dependencies. As we discussed earlier, this kind of control is crucial because it generates more organization for your project. Let's navigate to the principal parameters of the `composer.json` file:

- **Name**: This refers to the name of the component
- **Description**: This provides the description of the component
- **Require**: These are the dependencies of the project (the PHP version and the Magento libraries)
- **Type**: This describes the type of component (the theme or module)
- **Version**: This describes the version of the component
- **License**: This parameter describes the licenses applied on a component (Open Source License or Academic Free License)
- **Autoload**: This parameter defines the files and classes that will be autoloaded upon component activation.

CSS preprocessing with LESS

Before applying CSS in the CompStore Magento theme, it is important to study CSS behavior in the Magento system. The stylesheets in Magento 2.0 are preprocessed and compiled to CSS using the **LESS** technology. LESS (`http://lesscss.org/`) is a CSS preprocessor that extends the CSS traditional features by including variables and functions to generate a powerful CSS code and saves the time in maintaining the code.

All the `.less` files that you will save in your theme are compiled by the LESS engine but you will always declare `.css` in the Magento theme frontend. Here are a couple of examples:

- Frontend declaration: `<css src="css/styles.css" />`
- Root source file: `<Magento _theme_dir>/web/css/styles.less`

For further information, access the Magento 2.0 official documentation at `http://goo.gl/XLkOcQ`.

Applying new CSS to the CompStore theme

A CompStore theme inherits the Luma theme, which in turn inherits a blank theme, as shown here:

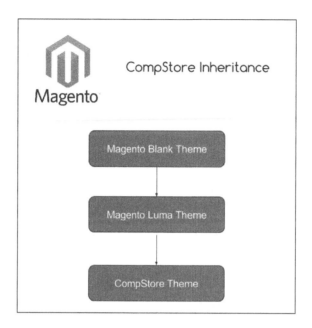

Once you have to make changes in CompStore in order to customize the new theme, you can think about the functionalities already available in the other themes to apply your changes.

The `vendor` directory under the Magento 2.0 root directory handles all the native Magento modules and themes. The Magento blank and Luma themes, which you have been working on until now, are available in `vendor/magento/theme-frontend-blank` and `vendor/magento/theme-frontend-luma`, respectively. So, the CompStore theme "receives" all the features of the themes under these folders. It's important to fix these basic concepts to understand the context that you inserted when you developed a Magento theme solution.

Once you have a solid concept about the behavior, let's create a custom `.css` file for the CompStore theme:

1. Copy the `packt/vendor/magento/theme-frontend-blank/web/css/_styles.less` file to the `packt/app/design/frontend/Packt/compstore/web/css` location

2. Open the copied file and insert an `import` command as the following example:

```
@import 'source/lib/_lib.less';
@import 'source/_sources.less';
@import 'source/_components.less';
@import 'source/compstore.less';
```

3. Save the file.

4. Now, open your favorite code editor and create the `compstore.less` file under the `packt/app/design/frontend/compstore/web/css/source` directory and type this code:

```
@color-compstore: #F6F6F6;


body{
background: @color-compstore;
}
```

5. Using override, let's change the product page color schema by creating the `_theme.less` file under the `packt/app/design/frontend/compstore/web/css/source` directory. Execute the following:

```
//Change color of elements in Product Page
@color-catalog: #4A96AD;
@page__background-color: @color-catalog;
@sidebar__background-color: @color-gray40;
@primary__color: @color-gray80;
@border-color__base: @color-gray76;
@link__color: @color-gray56;
@link__hover__color: @color-gray60;
@button__color: @color-gray20;
@button__background: @color-gray80;
@button__border: 1px solid @border-color__base;
@button-primary__background: @color-orange-red1;
@button-primary__border: 1px solid @color-orange-red2;
@button-primary__color: @color-white;
@button-primary__hover__background: darken(@color-orange-red1,
5%);
@button-primary__hover__border: 1px solid @color-orange-red2;
@button-primary__hover__color: @color-white;
@navigation-level0-item__color: @color-gray80;
@submenu-item__color: @color-gray80;
@navigation__background: @color-gray40;
@navigation-desktop-level0-item__color: @color-gray80;
@navigation-desktop-level0-item__hover__color: @color-gray34;
```

```
@navigation-desktop-level0-item__active__color: @navigation-
desktop-level0-item__color;
@tab-control__background-color: @page__background-color;
@form-element-input__background: @color-gray89;
@form-element-input-placeholder__color: @color-gray60;
@header-icons-color: @color-gray89;
@header-icons-color-hover: @color-gray60;
```

With the `compstore.less` and `_theme.less` files, the background and product page colors will change according to the new proposal of the CompStore theme.

Creating the CompStore logo

You can create a new logo for learning purposes using the **Logomakr** free online service (`http://logomakr.com/`). It's a pretty easy tool.

I created this logo for the CompStore theme using Logomakr:

My CompStore proposal of the logo was made in Logomakr, which is a solution developed by **Webalys** (`http://www.streamlineicons.com`) and **FlatIcon** (`http://www.flaticon.com`) and licensed under **Creative Commons by 3.0** (`http://creativecommons.org/licenses/by/3.0`). If you use this solution for other projects, don't forget to give the due credit to Logomakr.

After finishing the logo, save it under the `app/design/frontend/Packt/compstore/Magento_Theme/web/images/logo.png`path.

You can feel free to use your own solution for logo instead of using Logomakr.

Applying the theme

As you learned in the previous chapter, it's time to activate the new theme. Activate the CompStore Electronics theme in the Admin area (`http://localhost/packt/admin_packt`) to see the following result:

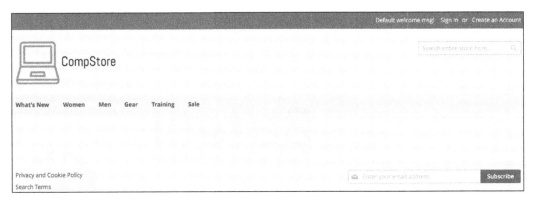

Sometimes, when you update in the Magento structure or activate a new theme, you need to deploy the theme and module changes. If you want to deploy your changes, follow these steps:

1. Open the terminal or command prompt.

2. Delete the `packt/pub/static/frontend/<Vendor>/<theme>/<locale>` directory.

3. Delete the `var/cache` directory.

4. Delete the `var/view_preprocessed` directory.

5. Then, access the `packt/bin` directory.

6. Run the php `magento setup:static-content:deploy` command.

7. In some cases, it is necessary to give `write` permissions again to the directories.

Creating CompStore content

Once the new theme is activated, it's time to handle the content by creating some options and configuring the products and categories.

To create new categories, you will need access the Admin area (`http://localhost/packt/admin_packt`) and follow this recipe:

1. Navigate to the **Products | Categories** menu.
2. Delete all the subcategories of **Default Category** by clicking on them and pressing the **Delete Category** button.
3. Create three new subcategories of **Default Category** named **Notebook**, **Desktops**, and **Peripherals**. Be sure to set to **Yes** the **Include in Navigation Menu** option for each category.

In the Add Category option, you have option to fill the **Description**, **Page Title**, and **Meta Information** areas for SEO purposes, as shown in the following screenshot:

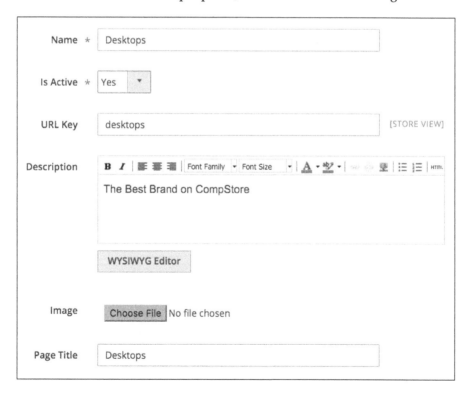

To create new products, you will need access to the Admin area (`http://localhost/packt/admin_packt`) and follow this recipe:

1. Access the Admin area (`http://localhost/packt/admin_packt`) and navigate to **Products | Catalog**.
2. Click on the **Add Product** button.
3. In the **New Product** page, enter all the required **Product Information** input.
4. Set the values of **Price** and **Quantity** categories.
5. Choose an image to upload.
6. Choose **In Stock** for the **Stock Availability** field.
7. Choose **Main Website** in the **Websites** tab.
8. Save your new product.
9. You can add three to nine products for testing purposes.

ID ↑	Thumbnail	Name	Type	Attribute Set	SKU	Price	Quantity	Visibility
2055		Printer 3	Simple Product	Default	Printer3	$80.00	10.0000	Catalog, Search
2054		Printer 2	Simple Product	Default	Printer 2	$80.00	10.0000	Catalog, Search
2053		Printer 1	Simple Product	Default	Printer 1	$80.00	10.0000	Catalog, Search
2052		Desktop 3	Simple Product	Default	Desktop3	$500.00	10.0000	Catalog, Search

Magento has a **widget** management system that allows the flexibility of the content. The widget helps create a specific list of new products in the home page. To create a new widget, follow these steps:

1. Navigate to **Content | Widgets**
2. Click on the **Add Widget** button
3. Then, in the **StoreFront** properties, perform the following:
    1. Select **CMS Static Block** as **Type** and **Compstore Electronics** as **Design Theme**.
    2. Type Home Page in the **Widget title** field.

3. Select the **All Store Views** option.

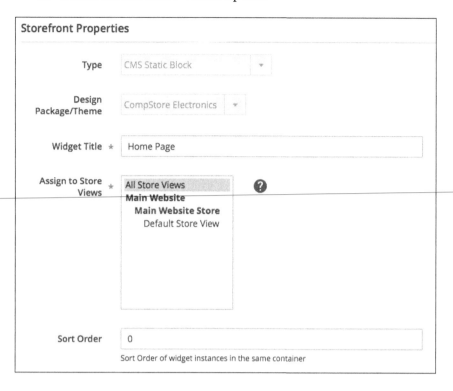

4. In **Layout Updates**, select the following options:
   ° For the **Display on** field, select the **Specified Page** option
   ° In the **Page** field, select the **CMS Home Page** option
   ° In the **Container** field, select the **Main Content Area** option
   ° The **Template** field should be **CMS Static Block Default Template**

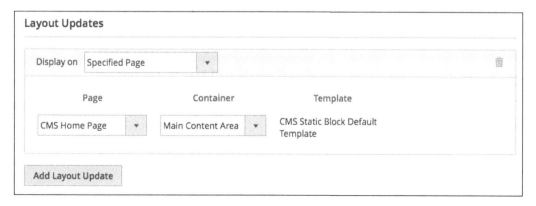

4. In **Widget Options**, perform the following:

    1. Select **Home Page Block**.

    2. Then, click on the **Save** button.

The default block configuration contains the images and products of the Luma theme. Let's change it via the following steps:

1. Navigate to **Content | Blocks**.

2. Click to edit **Home Page Block**

3. In the **Content** field, enter the following HTML code:

```
<div class="blocks-promo">
<a class="block-promo home-main" href="{{store url=""}}notebook.
html">
<img src="{{media url="wysiwyg/home-main.jpg"}}" alt="" />
<span class="content bg-white"><span class="info">New Desktop
available!</span>
<strong class="title">New Brands</strong>
<span class="action more button">Shop New Desktop</span> </span>
</a>
</div>
<div class="content-heading">
<h2 class="title">New Products</h2>
<p class="info">Here is what`s trending on CompStore now</p>
```

4. Position the cursor under the last line of the HTML code and click on the **Insert Widget** icon, as shown in the following screenshot:

5. Select **Catalog Products List** as **Widget Type**.

6. Select all the categories created earlier in the **Conditions** field.

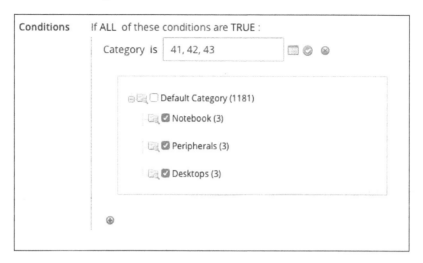

7. Click on the **Insert Widget** button.
8. If you prefer, you can change the image of the block.
9. Finally, click on the **Save Block** button.

Go to the Home page to see the final result:

Customizing Magento 2.0 templates

Magento works with .phtml template files to generate the view layer for the users. The modules and themes in Magento have its specific group of .phtml files to show data to the users. Let's create a custom template example in the CompStore theme to see how it works:

1. Create the Magento_Catalog directory under the compstore theme directory.

2. Copy the contents of vendor/magento/module_catalog/view/frontend/templates to app/design/frontend/Packt/compstore.

3. Then, open the app/design/frontend/Packt/compstore/Magento_Catalog/templates/product/view/addto.phtml file in your favorite code editor.

4. Go to Line 17 and enter the following code:

   ```
   <div><h2>Buy in CompStore!!!</h2></div>
   ```

5. Save the file.

6. Delete the var/view_preprocessed/ and pub/static/frontend/Packt/compstore/ directories.

7. Deploy static content files by running the php magento setup:static-content:deploy command.

8. If necessary, give write permission to the pub directory.

Navigate to the product page to see the result, as in the following screenshot:

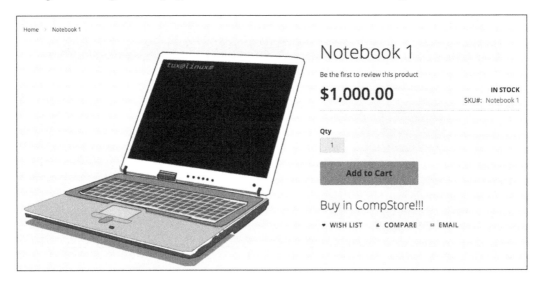

Summary

With the content learned in this chapter, you can now develop your own themes and customize solutions. The modern developer creates tools that can maximize the quality and minimize the effort to develop.

As a suggestion, try to read *Chapter 4, Magento 2.0 Theme Development – the Developers' Holy Grail*, again to create specific Magento pages and layout rules for the CompStore theme. You have uncountable possibilities to develop quality themes for Magento e-commerce and a great solid path to specialize more and more.

Now that you have all the tools to develop a theme for Magento, we will start discovering how to write Magento extensions by programming specific solutions in the next chapter.

6
Write Magento 2.0 Extensions – a Great Place to Go

In the previous chapter, we created a custom Magento 2.0 theme called CompStore. However, what do you think about extending our Magento expertise by creating our own extension? In this chapter, we will create a new extension called **TweetsAbout**, add a brand new functionality in our theme, learn the main concepts of Magento extension development, and take a look at how the extension packaging process works.

The following topics will be covered in this chapter:

- Magento development overview
- The Zend framework basics
- The Magento 2.0 extension structure
- The Twitter REST API
- Twitter OAuth
- Magento extension project – TweetsAbout

Magento development overview

Magento is an MVC-based application divided into modules. Each module has a specific job inside Magento, following a mature software pattern. For example, Magento has a specific module to control product shipping. This kind of approach is very important to create new functionalities and have the flexibility and modularity to extend its power.

Using the Zend framework

According to *Zend Framework Case Study* available at `https://www.zend.com/topics/Magento-CS.pdf`, the Magento project chose to go with industry-standard PHP and the Zend framework because of the extremely simple, object-oriented, and flexible solution that encapsulates best practices and agile testing methodologies and that would result in a very rapid development of enterprise-grade web applications.

Using the Zend framework as the main pillar in the Magento project definitely includes the following advantages:

- Magento contributors around the world know the Zend framework
- There is great web services support to integrate Magento with different software solutions in order to share data
- The MVC design pattern helps organize project development

With the Zend framework, Magento has great flexibility in creating and customizing modules, developing new features for the system, and maintaining the core code.

A basic understanding of Zend components could be interesting for developers to take advantage of this great MVC framework.

You can learn more about Zend framework at `http://framework.zend.com/`.

Magento 2.0 extension structure

Magento 2.0 is a modular system as you can see. That is why it is important to maintain all the code organized, and it couldn't be different with Magento extensions. In previous chapters you saw all the directory structure of Magento, but now let's give special attention to the basic Magento module file structure:

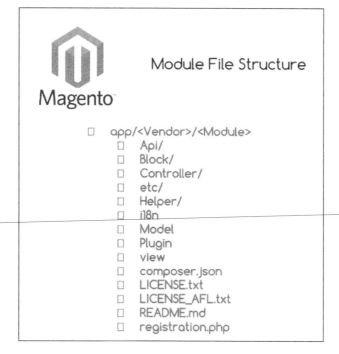

In order to create a new extension according to the preceding image, we must create the same directory structure. However, how will they interact with the Magento system?

Some of these directories have an important role to play in the Magento system. They are directories that are responsible for providing basic functionalities and coupling between modules and the Magento system:

- `Block`: Blocks are View classes that are responsible for providing visualization layers between the logical and frontend layer.

- `Controller`: These control all the actions of the Magento. Web servers process the requests and Controller redirects them to specific modules according to the URL.

- `etc`: This stores all the module XML configuration files.

- `Helper`: This stores auxiliary classes that provide forms, validators, and formatters, which are commonly used in business logic.

- `Model`: This stores all business logic and the access layer to the data.

- `Setup`: Setup classes are classes that control installation and upgrading functionalities.

The other directories support additional configurations and implementations of the module; these are as follows:

- `Api`: This directory contains classes to control the API's layers
- `i18n`: This directory contains files responsible for translating (internationalization) the module view layer
- `Plugin`: This directory handles plugins if necessary
- `view`: This directory handles all the template and layout files

The files presented in the root directory are files on which you worked before. The `LICENSES` and `README` files are those available for extension distribution purposes.

Developing your first Magento extension

Now, you have a general concept of creating a new extension for Magento. As a scenario to our development, we will create a simple extension called TweetsAbout to communicate with Twitter via the API and get the latest tweets with the `#magento`, `#packtpub`, and `#php` hashtags.

We will have two simple pages; the first will show a link to the results, and the second will show the tweets.

Let's get to work!

The Twitter REST API

Representational State Transfer (REST) is an architecture created to provide a simple communication channel between different applications over the Internet using mainly the HTTP protocol. It is the hottest data technology nowadays. **Facebook**, **Google**, **Twitter**, and a lot of huge companies have adopted REST applications. With REST APIs, you can read, post, and delete data.

Twitter has a specific format to spread its data on the Web in order to create great integration with different kinds of applications that consume its service. According to **Twitter Developers Documentation** available at `https://dev.twitter.com/rest/public`, Twitter REST APIs provide programmatic access to read and write Twitter data. You can author a new Tweet, read an author profile or follower data, and more. The REST API identifies Twitter applications and users using Oauth, and the responses are available in JSON.

Before beginning to code the Magento extension, let's create an account on Twitter Developer to authenticate our new application on the Twitter platform.

Create a new account in **Twitter** (`https://twitter.com/`) if you don't have one and access the **Twitter Developer page** (`https://dev.twitter.com/`), as in the following screenshot:

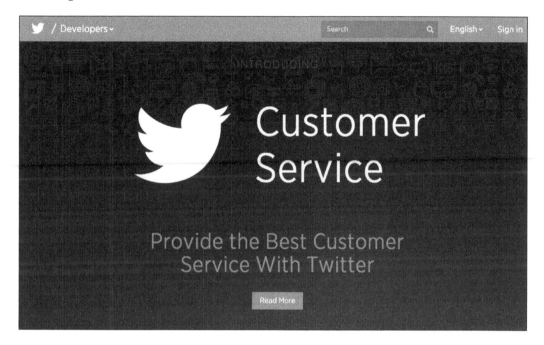

We have a lot of options on the developer's website, such as gathering real-time data, **crashlytics**, and **mopub**. I strongly suggest that you take a good look at these tools later.

So, let's create a new application to consume Twitter services. Access the URL `https://apps.twitter.com/` to create a new Twitter application. In order to use Twitter's public API services, you need to identify your application by generating a token and a secret key.

You can create a new application by clicking on the **Create New App** button and filling in the form with the following required fields:

- **Name**: Choose a unique name for your app
- **Description**: Describe your app
- **Website**: Provide a personal website/URL

Accept the **Developer Agreement** to finish your app registration and click on the **Create your Twitter Application** button.

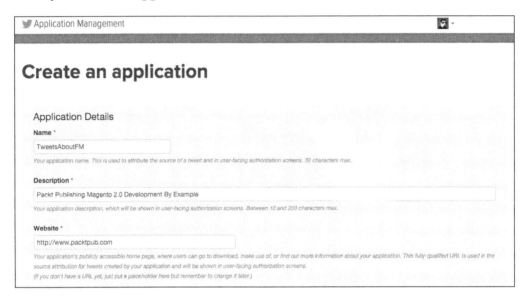

You can access your application's configurations by clicking on the name of your application. Later on in this chapter, we will discuss how to get the right credentials to integrate our application with Twitter.

Now, we can finally start our Magento 2.0 extension solution.

The TweetsAbout module structure

Create the following basic directory structure for the project:

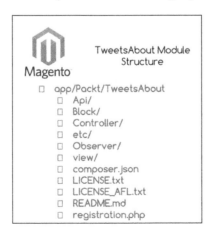

Using TwitterOAuth to authenticate our extension

The **TwitterOAuth** (`https://twitteroauth.com/`) library provides communication with Twitter via an API. In the TweetsAbout project, this kind of communication is essential for the final proposal of our extension solution. TwitterOAuth is the most popular PHP library to use with the TwitterOAuth REST API.

This project is also available on **GitHub** (`https://github.com/abraham/twitteroauth`), as shown in the following screenshot:

To install TwitterOAuth on the TweetsAbout extension, follow this recipe:

1. Open the terminal or command prompt.
2. Under the `packt/app/code/Packt/TweetsAbout/Api` directory, run the `composer require abraham/twitteroauth` command.

3. Access `https://apps.twitter.com/`, click on your application, and click on the **Keys and Access Tokens** tab to get the following:
   ○ **Consumer Key (API Key)**
   ○ **Consumer Secret (API Secret)**
   ○ **Access Token**
   ○ **Access Token Secret**

We'll need these credentials to use on our extension later.

Developing the module

To start the module development, we will declare the basic module configurations. Open your favorite code editor, create a new file called `module.xml`, and save the file in `app/code/Packt/TweetsAbout/etc`. Enter this code in the file:

```xml
<?xml version="1.0"?>
    <config xmlns:xsi="http://www.w3.org/2001/XMLSchema-instance" xsi:no
NamespaceSchemaLocation="urn:magento:framework:Module/etc/module.xsd">
        <module name="Packt_TweetsAbout" setup_version="2.0.0"/>
    </config>
```

Magento 2.0 works with **Uniform Resource Names** (**URN**) schema validation to reference XML declarations, as you can observe in the `<config>` tag. The `module.xsd` file works by validating whether your module declaration follows the module declaration schema.

The `<module>` tag contains the vendor and module name. Always follow this example of module name declaration: `Vendor_Module`.

Under `app/code/Packt/TweetsAbout/etc/frontend`, create two new files, as follows:

• `routes.xml`
• `events.xml`

The `routes.xml` file contains the following code:

```xml
<?xml version="1.0"?>
<config xmlns:xsi="http://www.w3.org/2001/XMLSchema-instance" xsi:noNa
mespaceSchemaLocation="urn:magento:framework:App/etc/routes.xsd">
    <router id="standard">
        <route id="tweetsabout" frontName="tweetsabout">
            <module name="Packt_TweetsAbout" />
```

```
            </route>
        </router>
</config>
```

The `routes.xml` file tells Magento where to look for the controllers (TweetsAbout/
Controller) when the URL `http://localhost/packt/tweetsabout` is accessed
(MVC).

The `events.xml` file contains the following code:

```
<?xml version="1.0"?>
<config xmlns:xsi="http://www.w3.org/2001/XMLSchema-instance" xsi:noNa
mespaceSchemaLocation="urn:magento:framework:Event/etc/events.xsd">
    <event name="page_block_html_topmenu_gethtml_before">
        <observer name="Packt_TweetsAbout_observer" instance="Packt\
TweetsAbout\Observer\Topmenu" />
    </event>
</config>
```

The `events.xml` file declares an **Observer** event handler in the module, and this
file has the mission of configuring a new TweetsAbout top menu link to access the
module in the frontend. Observer listens to events triggered by the user or system.
The `<event>` tag gets basic information of the top menu Block to be handled later in
the PHP code, and the `<observer>` tag declares the `Topmenu` observer class. In this
chapter, we will take a look at how the `Topmenu` class works. For now, it's important
to declare this option.

For further information about Observer, access the Magento official documentation
at `http://goo.gl/0CTzmn`.

Now, it is time to create the `registration.php` file under the root directory of
TweetsAbout. Run the following code:

```
<?php
\Magento\Framework\Component\ComponentRegistrar::register(
    \Magento\Framework\Component\ComponentRegistrar::MODULE,
    'Packt_TweetsAbout',
    __DIR__
);
```

The `registration.php` file has the same role as that of theme registration in
Magento System.

Create the `composer.json` file under the root directory of TweetsAbout via the following code:

```json
{
    "name": "packt/tweets-about",
    "description": "Example of Magento Module - Packt Publishing",
    "type": "magento2-module",
    "version": "1.0.0",
    "license": [
        "OSL-3.0",
        "AFL-3.0"
    ],
    "require": {
        "php": "~5.5.0|~5.6.0|~7.0.0",
        "magento/framework": "~100.0",
        "abraham/twitteroauth": "^0.6.2"
    },
    "autoload": {
        "files": [ "registration.php" ],
        "psr-4": {
            "Packt\\TweetsAbout\\": ""
        }
    },
    "extra": {
        "installer-paths": {
            "app/code/Packt/TweetsAbout/Api": ["abraham/twitteroauth"]
        }
    }
}
```

You can observe in the `composer.json` file the declaration of the TwitterOAuth project as a required package to our extension. Also, the file defines the installation directory.

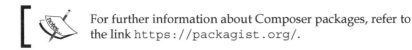

> For further information about Composer packages, refer to the link `https://packagist.org/`.

You can copy the `LICENSE.txt` and `LICENSE_AFL.txt` files from the Magento root directory to your `Packt/TweetsAbout` directory. The `README.md` file is responsible for storing information about the module's scope and some considerations for the purposes of publishing on GitHub (`http://github.com/`). You can feel free to create the `README.md` file as you wish.

For now, we have the module declaration and registration files. It's time to create the controllers to start giving some life to the TweetsAbout module.

Controllers

First, let's create a new file named Index.php. This file will control the access to the initial page of the module. Save it under app/code/Packt/TweetsAbout/ Controller/Index/ with the following code:

```php
<?php

namespace Packt\TweetsAbout\Controller\Index;

class Index extends \Magento\Framework\App\Action\Action{

    protected $resultPageFactory;

    public function __construct(
        \Magento\Framework\App\Action\Context $context,
        \Magento\Framework\View\Result\PageFactory
$resultPageFactory
    ) {
        $this->resultPageFactory = $resultPageFactory;
        parent::__construct($context);
    }

    public function execute(){
        return $this->resultPageFactory->create();
    }
}
```

Create another file named Index.php under app/code/Packt/TweetsAbout/ Controller/Magento/. This file will control the access to the Magento Tweets page of the module. Save it with the following code:

```php
<?php

namespace Packt\TweetsAbout\Controller\Magento;

class Index extends \Magento\Framework\App\Action\Action{

    protected $resultPageFactory;

    public function __construct(
        \Magento\Framework\App\Action\Context $context,
        \Magento\Framework\View\Result\PageFactory
$resultPageFactory
```

```
    ) {
        $this->resultPageFactory = $resultPageFactory;
        parent::__construct($context);
    }

    public function execute(){
        return $this->resultPageFactory->create();
    }
}
```

Create another file named `Index.php` under `app/code/Packt/TweetsAbout/Controller/Packt/`. This file will control the access to the `Packt` tweets page of the module. Save it with the following code:

```php
<?php

namespace Packt\TweetsAbout\Controller\Packt;

class Index extends \Magento\Framework\App\Action\Action{

    protected $resultPageFactory;

    public function __construct(
        \Magento\Framework\App\Action\Context $context,
        \Magento\Framework\View\Result\PageFactory
$resultPageFactory
    ) {
        $this->resultPageFactory = $resultPageFactory;
        parent::__construct($context);
    }

    public function execute(){
        return $this->resultPageFactory->create();
    }
}
```

Create another file named `Index.php` under `app/code/Packt/TweetsAbout/Controller/Php/`. This file will control the access to the PHP tweets page of the module. Save it with the following code:

```php
<?php

namespace Packt\TweetsAbout\Controller\Php;

class Index extends \Magento\Framework\App\Action\Action{
```

```
    protected $resultPageFactory;

    public function __construct(
        \Magento\Framework\App\Action\Context $context,
        \Magento\Framework\View\Result\PageFactory
$resultPageFactory
    ) {
        $this->resultPageFactory = $resultPageFactory;
        parent::__construct($context);
    }

    public function execute()
    {
        return $this->resultPageFactory->create();
    }
}
```

Magento 2.0 uses **namespaces** as a PHP standard recommendation (http://www.php-fig.org/psr/) to avoid name collisions between classes and to improve the readability of the code. So, in the namespace instruction, we will declare the class path to follow the **PSR-4 pattern** (http://www.php-fig.org/psr/psr-4/).

The extends functionality (inheritance) of \Magento\Framework\App\Action\Action provides a functionality to handle actions triggered by the URL access. For example, when the user enters the URL http://<magento_url>/tweetsabout, the routes.xml file redirects to the Index/Index.php controller to treat the user request made by accessing the URL.

The **dependency injection** of the __construct() method—\Magento\Framework\App\Action\Context $context and \Magento\Framework\View\Result\PageFactory $resultPageFactory—declares the initial construct of the Action class and the view layer to work with the template file.

 For further information about the dependency injection, access the Magento official documentation at http://goo.gl/jHFPTr.

Finally, the execute() method renders the layout. We will declare the layout files later on.

At this point, it's important to be familiar with PHP object-oriented programming (http://php.net/manual/en/language.oop5.php). I strongly suggest that you study the main concepts to increase the understanding of the book.

Blocks

Blocks in Magento 2.0 provide presentation logic for your view templates. In the TweetsAbout project, we will use two blocks to process the view template files.

Under the `app/code/Packt/TweetsAbout/Block` directory, create a file named `Index.php` with the following code:

```php
<?php

namespace Packt\TweetsAbout\Block;

class Index extends \Magento\Framework\View\Element\Template{

    public function getMagentoUrl(){
        return $this->getData('urlMagento');
    }

    public function getPHPUrl(){
        return $this->getData('urlPHP');
    }

    public function getPacktUrl(){
        return $this->getData('urlPackt');
    }
}
```

The three methods, `getMagentoUrl()`, `getPHPUrl()`, and `getPacktUrl()`, get data from layout declaration files to define a URL for each kind of controller and give it to the initial layout of the module.

Now, under the `app/code/Packt/TweetsAbout/Block` directory, create a file named `Tweets.php` with the following code:

```php
<?php
namespace Packt\TweetsAbout\Block;

require $_SERVER['DOCUMENT_ROOT'] . "/packt/app/code/Packt/
TweetsAbout/Api/vendor/autoload.php";
use Abraham\TwitterOAuth\TwitterOAuth;

class Tweets extends \Magento\Framework\View\Element\Template{

    private $consumerKey;
    private $consumerSecret;
```

```php
    private $accessToken;
    private $accessTokenSecret;

  public function searchTweets(){
    $connection = $this->twitterDevAuth();
    $result = $connection->get("search/tweets", array("q" =>$this-
>getData('hashtag'), "result_type"=>"recent", "count" => 10));

    return $result->statuses;
  }

  private function twitterDevAuth(){
    $this->consumerKey = YOUR_CONSUMER_KEY;
    $this->consumerSecret = YOUR_CONSUMER_SECRET;
    $this->accessToken = YOUR_ACCESS_TOKEN;
    $this->accessTokenSecret  = YOUR_ACCESS_TOKEN_SECRET;

    return new TwitterOAuth($this->consumerKey, $this-
>consumerSecret, $this->accessToken, $this->accessTokenSecret);
  }
 }
```

Here are some things to consider about the Tweets.php code:

- The required instruction is to call the autoload, and the use is to append the namespace of the TwitterOAuth library to work on our extension

- In the twitterDevAuth() method, you must enter the Twitter API credentials

- In the searchTweets() method, the $connection->get("search/tweets", array("q" =>$this->getData('hashtag'), "result_type"=>"recent", "count" => 10)) instruction works with the Twitter search API, getting the last 10 results of Twitter posts

Observer

Under the app/code/Packt/TweetsAbout/Observer directory, create the Topmenu. php file with the following code:

```php
<?php
namespace Packt\TweetsAbout\Observer;
use Magento\Framework\Event\Observer as EventObserver;
use Magento\Framework\Data\Tree\Node;
use Magento\Framework\Event\ObserverInterface;
```

```
class Topmenu implements ObserverInterface{

    /**
     * @param EventObserver $observer
     * @return $this
     */
    public function execute(EventObserver $observer)
    {

        $urlInterface = \Magento\Framework\App\
ObjectManager::getInstance()->get('Magento\Framework\UrlInterface');

        $active = strpos($urlInterface->getCurrentUrl(), "tweetsabout");


        /** @var \Magento\Framework\Data\Tree\Node $menu */
        $menu = $observer->getMenu();
        $tree = $menu->getTree();
        $data = [
            'name'      => __("TweetsAbout"),
            'id'        => 'tweetsmenu',
            'url'       => $urlInterface->getBaseUrl() .
'tweetsabout',
            'is_active' => $active
        ];
        $node = new Node($data, 'id', $tree, $menu);
        $menu->addChild($node);
        return $this;
    }
}
```

The `Topmenu.php` file dynamically creates a new top menu item for the TweetsAbout module by adding a node in the top menu link schema. The `\Magento\Framework\App\ObjectManager::getInstance()->get('Magento\Framework\UrlInterface')` instruction gets the base URL and the current URL to create a specific link to the TweetsAbout module. The `Topmenu` observer works with the **Document Object Model (DOM)** concept of nodes and trees dynamically.

Views

It's time to handle the presentation layer of the project. First, we will create the layout files (`.xml`) to handle template behavior and to pass arguments to the template via blocks. Every layout file is assigned by following this pattern: `<module_name>_<controller>_<controller_file>.xml`. This pattern allows the Magento system to assign the correct files according to its controller automatically.

Under the `app/code/Packt/TweetsAbout/view/frontend/layout` path, create the `tweetsabout_index_index.xml` file with the following code:

```
<?xml version="1.0"?>
<page xmlns:xsi="http://www.w3.org/2001/XMLSchema-instance"
layout="1column" xsi:noNamespaceSchemaLocation="urn:magento:framework:
View/Layout/etc/page_configuration.xsd">
    <head>
        <title>
            TweetsAbout Module
        </title>
    </head>
    <body>
        <referenceContainer name="content">
            <block class="Packt\TweetsAbout\Block\Index"
template="Packt_TweetsAbout::index.phtml">
                <arguments>
                    <argument name="urlMagento" xsi:type="url"
path="tweetsabout/magento" />
                    <argument name="urlPHP" xsi:type="url"
path="tweetsabout/php" />
                    <argument name="urlPackt" xsi:type="url"
path="tweetsabout/packt" />
                </arguments>
            </block>
        </referenceContainer>
    </body>
</page>
```

The `<block>` tag binds the `Index.php` Block to the `index.phtml` template, and the `<arguments>` tag transports three URL parameters to the Block. These parameters will be used in the `index.phtml` file.

Under the `app/code/Packt/TweetsAbout/view/frontend/layout` path, create the `tweetsabout_magento_index.xml` file with the following code:

```xml
<?xml version="1.0"?>
<page xmlns:xsi="http://www.w3.org/2001/XMLSchema-instance"
layout="1column" xsi:noNamespaceSchemaLocation="urn:magento:framework:
View/Layout/etc/page_configuration.xsd">
    <head>
        <title>
            TweetsAbout #Magento
        </title>
        <css src="Packt_TweetsAbout::css/source/module.css"/>
    </head>
    <body>
        <referenceContainer name="content">
            <block class="Packt\TweetsAbout\Block\Tweets"
template="Packt_TweetsAbout::tweets.phtml">
                <arguments>
                    <argument name="hashtag"
xsi:type="string">#magento</argument>
                </arguments>
            </block>
        </referenceContainer>
    </body>
</page>
```

Under the `app/code/Packt/TweetsAbout/view/frontend/layout` path, create the `tweetsabout_packt_index.xml` file with the following code:

```xml
<?xml version="1.0"?>
<page xmlns:xsi="http://www.w3.org/2001/XMLSchema-instance"
layout="1column" xsi:noNamespaceSchemaLocation="urn:magento:framework:
View/Layout/etc/page_configuration.xsd">
    <head>
        <title>
            TweetsAbout #Packtpub
        </title>
        <css src="Packt_TweetsAbout::css/source/module.css"/>
    </head>
    <body>
        <referenceContainer name="content">
```

```
                    <block class="Packt\TweetsAbout\Block\Tweets"
        template="Packt_TweetsAbout::tweets.phtml">
                        <arguments>
                            <argument name="hashtag"
        xsi:type="string">#packtpub</argument>
                        </arguments>
                    </block>
                </referenceContainer>
            </body>
        </page>
```

Under the `app/code/Packt/TweetsAbout/view/frontend/layout` path, create the `tweetsabout_php_index.xml` file with the following code:

```xml
<?xml version="1.0"?>
<page xmlns:xsi="http://www.w3.org/2001/XMLSchema-instance"
layout="1column" xsi:noNamespaceSchemaLocation="urn:magento:framework:
View/Layout/etc/page_configuration.xsd">
    <head>
        <title>
            TweetsAbout #PHP
        </title>
        <css src="Packt_TweetsAbout::css/source/module.css"/>
    </head>
    <body>
        <referenceContainer name="content">
            <block class="Packt\TweetsAbout\Block\Tweets"
template="Packt_TweetsAbout::tweets.phtml">
                <arguments>
                    <argument name="hashtag" xsi:type="string">#php</
argument>
                </arguments>
            </block>
        </referenceContainer>
    </body>
</page>
```

The `<css>` tag loads the CSS rules of the template. The `<block>` tag binds the `Tweets.php` Block to the `tweets.phtml` file. The `<argument name="hashtag">` tag transports the **hashtag** parameter to the `Tweets.php` Block to search the latest mentions of the specific hashtag in the Twitter database.

Now, let's create the `template` files.

Under the `app/code/Packt/TweetsAbout/view/frontend/templates` path, create the `index.phtml` file with the following code:

```
<h2>Recent TweetsAbout: </h2>
<ul>
  <li>
    <a href="<?php echo $block->escapeHtml($block->getMagentoUrl())
?>">
      <span><?php echo __('Magento')?></span>
    </a>
  </li>
  <li>
    <a href="<?php echo $block->escapeHtml($block->getPacktUrl()) ?>">
      <span><?php echo __('Packtpub')?></span>
    </a>
  </li>
  <li>
    <a href="<?php echo $block->escapeHtml($block->getPHPUrl()) ?>">
      <span><?php echo __('PHP')?></span>
    </a>
  </li>
</ul>
```

The `$block` object has access to the methods of `Block/Index.php`, and the URL of the pages build dynamically.

Under the `app/code/Packt/TweetsAbout/view/frontend/templates` path, create the `tweets.phtml` file with the following code:

```
<?php
  $tweets = $block->searchTweets();
?>

<?php foreach ($tweets as $tweet){ ?>
  <p class="tweet">
    <a href="<?php echo $tweet->user->url; ?>">
      <img src="<?php echo $tweet->user->profile_image_url; ?>"
alt="profile">
    </a>
```

```
    <b>Created: </b><?php echo $tweet->created_at; ?>
    <br />
    <br />

    <a href="<?php echo isset($tweet->entities->urls[0]->url) ?
$tweet->entities->urls[0]->url : "#"; ?>" target="_blank"><?php echo
$tweet->text;?></a>

  </p>
  <hr />
<?php } ?>
```

The `searchTweets()` method loads tweets according to the URL accessed, and PHP processes the data to show the results to the user.

CSS

Under the `app/code/Packt/TweetsAbout/view/frontend/web/css/source` path, create the `module.less` file with the following code:

```
.tweet {background-color: #878787; padding:15px; border:1px dotted}
.tweet a {color: #ffffff}
.tweet a:hover {text-decoration: underline;}
```

Deploying the module

To deploy the module, follow this recipe:

1. Open the terminal or command prompt.
2. Access the `packt/bin` directory.
3. Then, run the `php magento module:enable --clear-static-content Packt_TweetsAbout` command.
4. Run the `php magento setup:upgrade` command.
5. Next, run the `php magento setup:static-content:deploy` command.
6. In some cases, it is necessary to give `write` permissions again to the directories.

If everything goes alright, when you access the URL `http://localhost/packt`, you will see one link for the `TweetsAbout` extension in the topmost menu. Just click on it to see how the extension works. Take a look at the following screenshot:

You can navigate to the links to see how the pages work, as in the following screenshot:

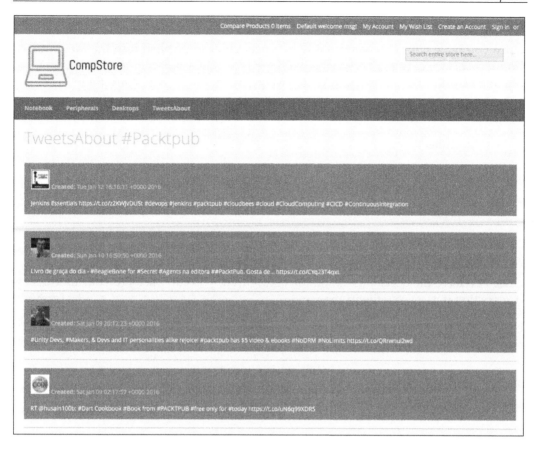

The extension gets the ten last tweets in real time with the date, picture, and post. It's really awesome to watch our work running!

For sure, this extension can get a lot better, but it is only a starting point for big achievements.

Magento Connect

Once you have your extension ready to work, you can publish it in the Magento Connect service (`http://www.magentocommerce.com/magento-connect`). Magento Connect is a service in which Magento members can share their open source or commercial extensions with Magento Community. The main contributions are generally based on the following:

- Modules
- Language packs
- Design interfaces
- Themes

Packaging and publishing your module

Once you have the `composer.json` file configured, you can package your module by compacting it as a `.zip` file in the `vendor-name_package-name-1.0.0.zip` format.

Upload the module in your personal account in GitHub, and Magento can retrieve it to publish.

For further information, it's strongly recommended that you to access the official documentation available on the Magento Developers official site at `http://devdocs.magento.com/guides/v2.0/extension-dev-guide/package_module.html`.

Summary

You worked on a lot in this chapter! Congratulations. Now, you have solid grasp of the concept in Magento 2.0 extension development. You can note that Magento development has strict rules, but once you learn the basics, you can master Magento with hard work and study. Keep the good work going!

As a suggestion, try to read the official documentation and do projects that demand more user interaction, such as the admin panel and development of dynamic formularies. You can even increase the power of TweetsAbout. The sky is the limit!

In the next chapter, we will start to work with Magento mobile by testing and configuring some great options. See you!

7
Go Mobile with Magento 2.0!

Nowadays e-commerce stores must be responsive and mobile friendly to increase sales according to the huge number of people using mobile devices to buy products and services. It's very important to know the right tools to provide a mobile-friendly Magento theme for your project. Let's go mobile with Magento!

The following topics will be covered in this chapter:

- Why mobile and responsive?
- Testing the website on different devices
- The Google Chrome DevTools device mode
- Responsive web designer tester extension
- Adjusting the CompStore theme for mobile devices
- Adjusting tweets for mobile devices

According to a research called **State of Mobile Commerce Growing like a weed Q1 2015** conducted by **Criteo** (http://www.criteo.com/), a digital marketing company, mobile accounts for 29% of e-commerce transactions in the US and 34% globally. By the end of 2015, mobile share is forecast to reach 33% in the US and 40% globally. This research is available at http://www.criteo.com/media/1894/criteo-state-of-mobile-commerce-q1-2015-ppt.pdf.

This is one of the main reasons for which all Magento developers must create responsive designs. We started this process indirectly by creating a new theme with **Webcomm Magento Boilerplate**. Despite its basic mobile support, we have to make some adjustments to create a completely responsive Magento theme. Let's return to work!

Testing the website on different devices

In order to test your website in different devices and, consequently, different screen sizes, it is recommended to use a specific software or service to simulate the screen sizes of devices. If you perform a search on the web, you may find a great number of online test tools, but these tools work only with published websites. Our Magento site works, for now, on our local development environment.

To take advantage of our local development environment, let's work with the **Google Chrome DevTools Device Mode** and the **Responsive Web Designer Tester** extensions. In this book, we'll have two options to work with mobile theme development. You choose both of them!

If you don't have Google Chrome installed, download it from the URL `https://www.google.com/intl/en/chrome/browser/desktop/` to install it on your operating system.

The Google Chrome DevTools device mode

Google Chrome DevTools is a native tool of Google Chrome that provides a bunch of tools for web developers. By working with DevTools, you can optimize your frontend code, including HTML, CSS, and JavaScript.

Before accessing the DevTools extensions, access your Magento CompStore website at the `http://localhost/packt` URL.

To access DevTools, in the Google Chrome browser, follow these steps:

1. Click on the Google Chrome menu.
2. Click on the **More Tools** option.

3. Click on the **Developer Tools** option.

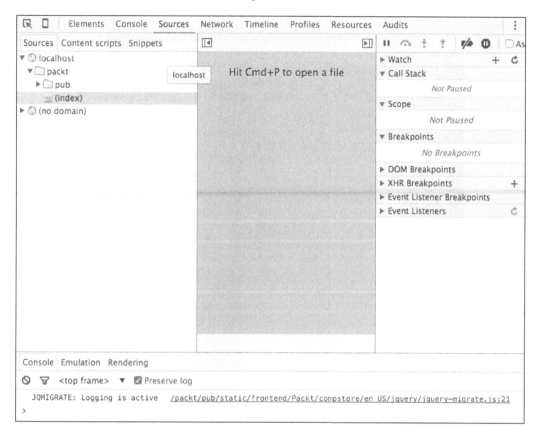

Now, you can see the **DevTools** window, as in the preceding screenshot.

To activate **Device Mode**, click on the smartphone icon next to the **Elements** menu item. Now, you can see the page rendering with different options, as in the following screenshot:

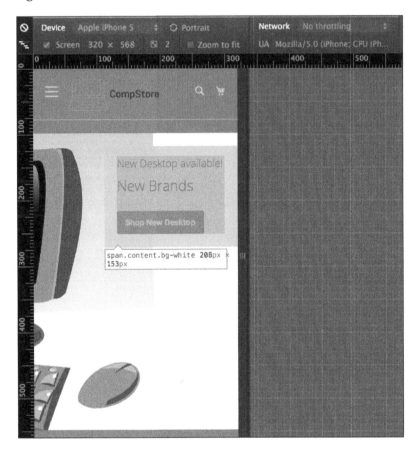

According to the Google DevTools official page available at https://developers. google.com/web/tools/chrome-devtools/iterate/device-mode/, you can use the DevTools device mode to do the following:

- Test your responsive designs
- Visualize and inspect CSS queries
- Use a network emulator to evaluate site performance
- Enhance your debugging workflow

The DevTools extension has the following options to enhance developer experience:

- **Device preset**
- **Network connectivity**
- **Inspecting media queries**
- **View CSS**
- **Add custom devices**

Changing the device preset

To change the device preset, click on the **Device** options:

You can choose from among iPhone, Google Nexus, Samsung Galaxy, and Blackberry, and you can create custom devices to test the screen size.

Network connectivity

This option emulates various network conditions of your website access.

Inspecting media queries

The media queries are responsible for defining the CSS rule for each screen size. You can access all of these using DevTools. To access media queries, click on the icon in the upper-left corner:

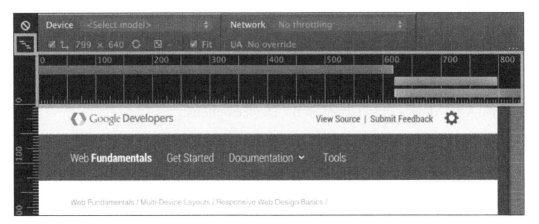

Viewing CSS

Right-click on a bar to view the CSS media query rule. You can make adjustments in the CSS code:

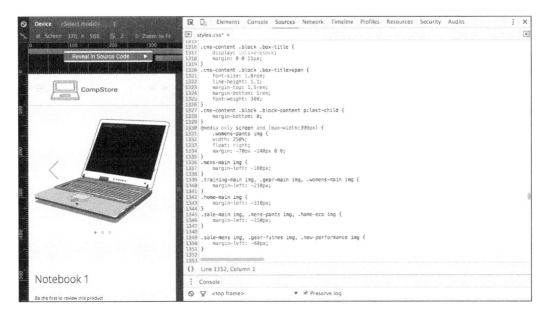

Adding custom devices

To create custom devices, follow these steps:

1. In the **Developer Tools** topmost menu, click on **Settings**.
2. Click on the **Devices** tab.
3. Then, click on the **Add Custom Device** button.
4. Fill the form according your need.
5. Next, click on the **Add Device** button.

Now, you have your own device to test your code.

Responsive Web Designer tester

Now, open the Google Chrome browser and navigate to the address
`https://chrome.google.com/webstore/category/apps` to access
Chrome Web Store. Conduct a search to find the **Responsive Web Designer
Tester** extension and then add the extension to Google Chrome, as follows:

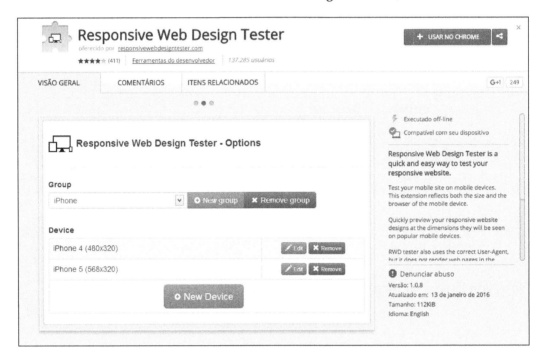

Great work! Now, let's take a look at how this extension works. On your browser,
go to your Magento local site, also known as CompStore, by accessing `http://
localhost/packt`. Remember that you have to turn on Apache Service in XAMMP
to test the local website.

Click on the button of the **Responsive Web Designer Tester** extension shown on the
right-hand side of your screen (generally near the end of the browser address bar)
and select the **iPhone 5 — Portrait** option for the first test:

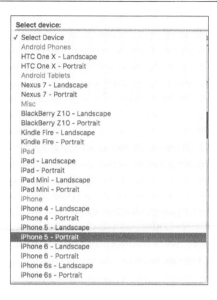

After you select the device, you will see a pop-up window having the size of iPhone 5 screen. Navigating on the page, you will see also that the layout is not fully responsive. We have some issues in the home page presentation:

Now we have a tool to test site behavior between the different devices. It is time to make our CompStore theme 100% compatible with multiple devices!

Adjusting the CompStore theme for mobile devices

Both the Magento 2.0 native themes, Blank and Luma, use **Responsive Web Design (RWD)** to provide good visualization in different devices, such as desktops, tablets, and mobiles.

In spite of the fact that the CompStore theme inherited the Luma theme, you can customize the template and CSS codes, as we discussed in *Chapter 6, Write Magento 2.0 Extensions – a Great Place to Go*. So, what do you think about improving the CompStore theme to make it more user friendly?

The actual mobile version of CompStore has some differences in the desktop version, including colors, elements positioning, and image size. Before creating some mobile standards for the CompStore theme, it's important to fix some CSS responsive design concepts of Magento. Let's get to work!

The Magento 2.0 responsive design

To handle accessibility for different devices, the Magento 2.0 native themes (Blank and Luma) work with an RWD engine, as we discussed in the *Chapter 4, Magento 2.0 Theme Development – the Developers' Holy Grail*, and *Chapter 5, Creating a Responsive Magento 2.0 Theme*. The stylesheets engine provided by the LESS preprocessor is the main utility responsible for this design approach.

The Magento 2.0 native themes were built based on the **Magento UI library**. The Magento UI library works with **CSS 3 media queries** to render a page with predefined rules according to the device, which requests the page. An example of media queries would be one that applies a specific rule for screens with a maximum width of 640 px; take a look at the following code:

```
@media only screen and (max-width: 640px) {
    ...
}
```

With media queries, the themes apply **breakpoints** to handle different screen-width rules for different screen sizes of devices in a progression scale of pixels, as follows:

- 320 px (mobile)
- 480 px (mobile)
- 640 px (tablet)
- 768 px (tablet to desktop)
- 1024 px (desktop)
- 1440 px (desktop)

For further information about media queries, refer to the **W3C** official documentation available at `https://www.w3.org/TR/css3-mediaqueries/`.

The Magento UI

The Magento 2.0 system works with the LESS CSS preprocessor to extend the features of CSS and enable the opportunity to create theme inheritance with minimal and organized effort. With this premise, to help theme developers, we have the Magento UI library in Magento 2.0.

The Magento UI library is based on LESS and provides a set of components to develop themes and frontend solutions:

- Actions toolbar
- Breadcrumbs
- Buttons
- Drop-down menus
- Forms
- Icons
- Layout
- Loaders
- Messages
- Pagination
- Popups
- Ratings
- Sections
- Tabs and accordions

- Tables
- Tooltips
- Typography
- A list of theme variables

Another important resource of the Magento UI and of LESS is the **mixin** capability. The mixin allows developers to group style rules to work with different devices.

For example, consider that you declared the following CSS code in one determined file:

```
.media-width(@extremum, @break) when (@extremum = 'max') and (@break =
@screen__m) {
    .example-responsive-block {
        background: #ffc;
    }
    .example-responsive-block:before {
        content: 'Mobile styles ';
        font-weight: bold;
    }
}
```

Then, you executed this CSS code in a different file:

```
.media-width(@extremum, @break) when (@extremum = 'min') and (@break =
@screen__m) {
    .example-responsive-block {
        background: #ccf;
    }
    .example-responsive-block:before {
        content: 'Desktop styles ';
        font-weight: bold;
    }
}
```

In spite of the two files declaring a mixin named `.media-width` to the `.example-responsive-block` class in different files, the mixin allows LESS to make a single query, grouping the rules instead of making multiple calls according to the device rule applied.

You can access the local Magento UI documentation by accessing the URL `http://<magento_local_url>/pub/static/frontend/Magento/blank/en_US/css/docs/responsive.html`.

For further information about the Magento UI, take a look at the Magento official `readme.md` file available at `https://github.com/magento/magento2/blob/2.0.0/lib/web/css/docs/source/README.md`.

Implementing a new CSS mixin media query

First of all, let's take a look at the current mobile version of the CompStore theme. Using Chrome DevTools or Responsive Web Designer Tester, select an Apple iPhone 5 (portrait) device to test the site. You will probably be redirected to home page:

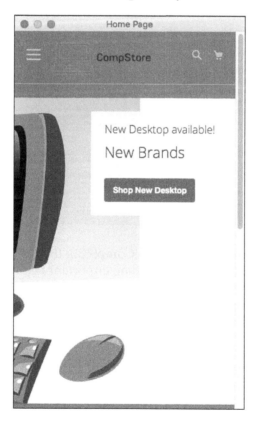

In spite of the previous adjustment in the CompStore theme, when a mobile device accesses a theme, CSS rules don't apply some important features, such as colors and the positioning of elements. As a suggestion, let's create a standard declaration of color approach and configure CSS to show only one product when the mobile device accesses the site. How can we implement these new features? Using media queries, of course!

In your favorite code editor, open the `compstore.less` file available under the `app/design/frontend/Packt/compstore/web/css/source` directory and use the following CSS 3 code:

```
@color-compstore: #F6F6F6;

body{
  background: @color-compstore;
```

```
    }

    .media-width(@extremum, @break) when (@extremum = 'max') and (@break =
    @screen__s) {
      body{
        background: @color-compstore;
      }
      .widget .block-promo img{
        height: 600px;
      }

      .products-grid .product-item {
        width: 100%;
        display: inline-block;
      }
    }

    .media-width(@extremum, @break) when (@extremum = 'min') and (@break =
    @screen__s) {
      body{
        background: @color-compstore;
      }
      .widget .block-promo img{
        height: 600px;
      }
      .products-grid .product-item {
        width: 100%;
        display: inline-block;
      }
    }
```

The Magento UI break points predefined variables to identify the scope of media queries, which are as follows:

- `@screen__xxs`: 320 px

- `@screen__xs`: 480 px

- `@screen__s`: 640 px

- `@screen__m`: 768 px

- `@screen__l`: 1024 px

- `@screen__xl`: 1440 px

So, in the CSS 3 new proposal, the media queries use the `@screen_s` variable to define the application of new rules. We will propose via mixin to change the background color, promo image size, and product size inside mobile rules for portrait and landscape purposes.

To apply the changes, follow this recipe:

1. Save the file.

2. Open the terminal or command prompt.

3. Delete the `packt/pub/static/frontend/<Vendor>/<theme>/<locale>` directory.

4. Delete the `var/cache` directory.

5. Then, delete the `var/view_preprocessed` directory.

6. Access the `packt/bin` directory.

7. Next, run the `php magento setup:static-content:deploy` command.

8. In some cases, it is necessary to give `write` permissions again to the directories.

Test the site again to get the new home page, as in the following screenshot:

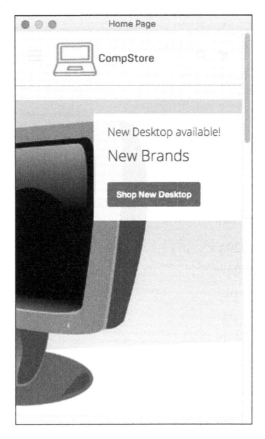

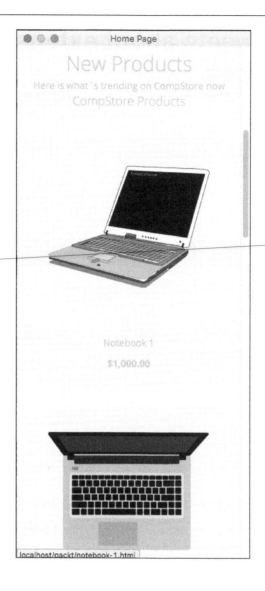

Adjusting tweets about extensions for mobile devices

The extension that we created in *Chapter 6, Write Magento 2.0 Extensions – a Great Place to Go*, tweets about extension and has the following appearance:

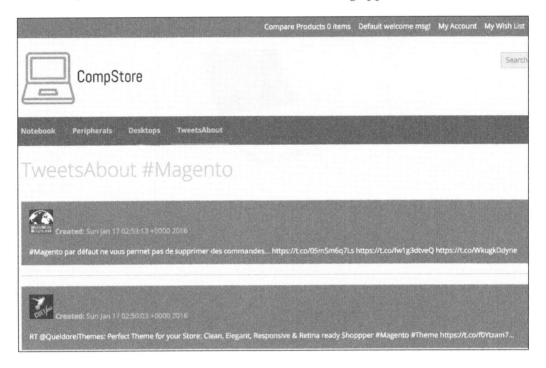

Let's improve the CSS extension rules to turn it into a mobile-friendly one.

Using Chrome DevTools or Responsive Web Designer Tester, select an Apple iPhone 5—portrait device to test our code optimization.

Open the `module.less` file available under the `packt/app/code/Packt/TweetsAbout/view/frontend/web/css/source` directory and add the following code:

```
/*Tweets About Style*/

@media (min-width: 960px){
#wrapper {
width: 90%;
max-width: 1100px;
```

```
min-width: 800px;
margin: 50px auto;
    }

  #columns {
    -webkit-column-count: 3;
    -webkit-column-gap: 10px;
    -webkit-column-fill: auto;
    -moz-column-count: 3;
    -moz-column-gap: 10px;
    -moz-column-fill: auto;
    column-count: 3;
    column-gap: 15px;
    column-fill: auto;
  }
}

.tweet {
    display: inline-block;
    background: #FEFEFE;
    border: 2px solid #FAFAFA;
    box-shadow: 0 1px 2px rgba(34, 25, 25, 0.4);
    margin: 0 2px 15px;
    -webkit-column-break-inside: avoid;
    -moz-column-break-inside: avoid;
    column-break-inside: avoid;
    padding: 15px;
    padding-bottom: 5px;
    background: -webkit-linear-gradient(45deg, #FFF, #F9F9F9);
    opacity: 1;

    -webkit-transition: all .2s ease;
    -moz-transition: all .2s ease;
    -o-transition: all .2s ease;
    transition: all .2s ease;
}

.tweetimg {
    width: 15%;
    display:block;
    float:left;
    margin: 0px 5px 0px 0px;
}

.tweet p {
    font: 12px/18px Arial, sans-serif;
```

```
    color: #333;
    margin: 0;
}

#columns:hover .img:not(:hover) {
    opacity: 0.4;
}
```

After saving the `module.less` file, change the `tweets.phtml` code available under `packt/app/code/Packt/TweetsAbout/view/frontend /templates`, change the file with this new code, and save it, as follows:

```
<?php
  $tweets = $block->searchTweets();
?>

<div id="wrapper">
  <div id="columns">
    <?php foreach ($tweets as $tweet){ ?>
      <div class="tweet">
        <p>
          <a href="https://twitter.com/intent/user?user_id=<?php echo
$tweet->user->id; ?>" target="_blank">
            <img src="<?php echo $tweets->user->profile_image_url; ?>"
alt="profile">
            <?php echo $tweet->user->name; ?>
          </a>
          <br />
          Created: <?php echo $tweets->created_at; ?>
          <br /><br />
          <a href="<?php echo isset($tweet->entities->urls[0]->url) ?
$tweet->entities->urls[0]->url : "#"; ?>" target="_blank"><?php echo
$tweet->text;?></a>
            <?php echo $tweets->text;?>
          </a>
        </p>
      </div>
    <?php } ?>
  </div>
</div>
```

To deploy the module update, follow this recipe:

1. Open the terminal or command prompt.
2. Access the `packt/bin` directory.

3. Then, run the `php magento module:enable --clear-static-content Packt_TweetsAbout` command.

4. Run the `php magento setup:upgrade` command.

5. Next, run the `php magento setup:static-content:deploy` command.

6. In some cases, it is necessary to give `write` permissions again to the directories (`var` and `pub`).

Now, test the tweets about extension by accessing `http://localhost/packt/tweetsabout` to see the new responsive look, as shown in the following screenshot:

If you activate DevTools and choose an iPhone 5 device, you will see a result similar to the following screenshot:

Summary

In this chapter, you learned about tools that provide you with a great environment to develop Magento frontend themes.

You also increased the power of CompStore CSS to handle access from specific mobile devices. Of course, you can modify the code constantly to have a better experience by fine-tuning in your code. However, this is only the beginning.

In the next chapter, we will start configuring our Magento software, on which we have been working until now, to improve its speed. We will installing solutions and configure the already native Magento options.

8
Speeding up Your Magento 2.0

Despite the existence of a great solution such as Zend Framework for its system, Magento 2.0 needs some fine tuning to get the best performance in order to provide the users with a better shopping experience. As you noted in the previous chapters, it is very important to focus on every aspect for successful e-commerce.

The following topics will be covered in this chapter:

- Magento Entity-Attribute-Value
- Indexing and re-indexing data
- Caching
- Selecting the right Magento hosting service
- Apache web server deflation
- Enabling the `expires` header
- PHP memory configuration
- Optimizing the MySQL server
- Cleaning the database log
- Minifying scripts
- CDN for Magento

Magento Entity-Attribute-Value

With a complex system architecture, Magento developers realized that a traditional development approach could be counterproductive for a scalable idea to implement an e-commerce solution.

Developers, therefore, decided to adopt the **Entity-Attribute-Value (EAV)** architecture approach.

This database structure embraces the Magento 2.0 complexity processes and variables and allows an unlimited numbers of attributes to any item, such as categories, products, costumers, addresses, and more.

The three main points of EAV can be described as follows:

- **Entity**: Data items are represented as entities. In the database, each entity has a record.

- **Attribute**: Many attributes could belong to a specific entity; for example, the customer entity has name, birth date, phone, and so on. In Magento, all the attributes are listed in a single table.

- **Value**: This is the value of each attribute. For example, customer is an entity that has an attribute called name with the value Fernando Miguel.

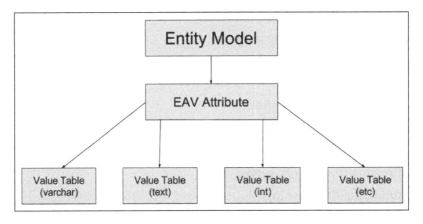

This book is a hands–on guide to Magento, but I strongly suggest you to read more about EAV in the Magento official documentation at `http://devdocs.magento.com/guides/v2.0/extension-dev-guide/attributes.html`.

Indexing and caching Magento

With the increase in content, images, and script demands for a better experience in e-commerce, we have to handle network consumption in order to provide fast access to our system. Search engines measure some technical points with their algorithms, and fast access is, of course, one of the requisites validated.

Magento has a complex architecture and works with MySQL database constant queries to show specific products information, render pages, and process checkouts. This high process volume demand can slow the download speed when your Magento 2.0 solution is in a production environment.

To improve the Magento 2.0 performance, we can use two important tools: **indexing** and **caching**.

Indexing and re-indexing data

In the Magento 2.0 life cycle, at a determined point, we will have considerable megabytes of data on the MySQL database, including information regarding products, orders, customers, and payments. To improve its performance, Magento uses indexed tables to provide faster lookups.

However, as your Magento 2.0 e-commerce grows, the indexation feature starts to lose performance too.

In order to correct this issue, you can precompile database relationships using the **flat table** option in Magento. This technique combines EAV relationships for categories and products in one table to increase the speed of queries. To enable this feature, you can follow these instructions:

1. Log in to your Magento backend (`http://localhost/packt/admin_packt`).

2. Go to **Stores | Configuration | Catalog**.

3. Expand the **Storefront** option and select **Yes** for both **Use Flat Category** and **Use Flat Catalog Product**.

4. Next, click on **Save Config**.

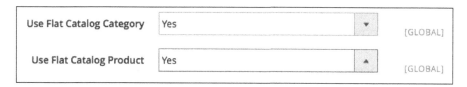

5. After the activation of the flat resource, you will probably get this Magento message:

> ⚠ One or more indexers are invalid. **Make sure your** Magento cron job **is running.**   ✕

If you make changes to your catalog, product, or some page that has a relationship with **indexers**, the Magento system needs to re-index the information to keep the flat table schema working. You can manage the indexers with the Magento command-line tool, as follows:

1. Open the terminal or command prompt.

2. Access the `packt/bin` directory. Then, run the `php magento indexer:reindex` command.

3. In some cases, it is necessary to give write permissions again to the directories.

```
Customer Grid index has been rebuilt successfully in 00:00:05
Product Flat Data index has been rebuilt successfully in 00:00:07
Category Flat Data index has been rebuilt successfully in 00:00:02
Category Products index has been rebuilt successfully in 00:00:00
Product Categories index has been rebuilt successfully in 00:00:00
Product Price index has been rebuilt successfully in 00:00:08
Product EAV index has been rebuilt successfully in 00:00:02
Stock index has been rebuilt successfully in 00:00:00
Catalog Search index has been rebuilt successfully in 00:00:04
Catalog Rule Product index has been rebuilt successfully in 00:00:03
Catalog Product Rule index has been rebuilt successfully in 00:00:02
```

The `reindex` command rebuilds all the product, catalog, customer, and stock information. The index feature enables a fast return of data once the system has no need to process any basic data, such as product price, every single time that the user accesses the store.

Did you notice in the preceding system message one issue about **Magento cron job**? Cron job allows you to automate this task and others to improve your efficiency. Let's take a look at how cron job works.

For further information about Magento indexing, take a look at the official Magento documentation at `http://devdocs.magento.com/guides/v2.0/extension-dev-guide/indexing.html`.

The Magento cron job

Magento has important system processes that are very important to maintain the system's working at its full potential. These processes need automated executions to handle the updates made by the user and administrator. That is the why this feature is critical to Magento.

Cron job works with UNIX systems and can schedule specific tasks to be executed in a predetermined time on the server. The following activities can be scheduled to execute on the Magento 2.0 system:

- The updating of currency rates
- Customer notifications
- The generation of Google sitemap
- Price rules
- Sending e-mails
- Re-indexing

To configure the cron job, follow this recipe.

Find the `php.ini` file path.

If you use XAMPP, as was suggested for a web server solution at the beginning of the book, you simply can use the `XAMPP/xamppfiles/etc/php.ini` path. If you use a Unix-based terminal, you can use the command to find the PHP configuration file. Perform the following steps:

1. Open the terminal.
2. Run the `sudo crontab -u magento_user -e` command; here, `magento_user` refers to your system's owner.
3. Enter with the following instructions in the text editor that will show up:

   ```
   */1 * * * * php -c <php-ini-file-path> <your Magento install dir>/
   bin/magento cron:run
   */1 * * * * php -c <php-ini-file-path> <your Magento install dir>/
   update/cron.php
   */1 * * * * php -c <php-file-path> <your Magento install dir>/bin/
   magento setup:cron:run
   ```

   Here's an example:

   ```
   */1 * * * * php -c /Applications/XAMPP/xamppfiles/etc/php.ini /
   Applications/XAMPP/xamppfiles/etc/php.ini /Applications/XAMPP/
   htdocs/packt/bin/magento cron:run
   ```

```
*/1 * * * * php -c /Applications/XAMPP/xamppfiles/etc/php.ini /
Applications/XAMPP/xamppfiles/etc/php.ini /Applications/XAMPP/
htdocs/packt/update/cron.php
*/1 * * * * php -c /Applications/XAMPP/xamppfiles/etc/php.ini /
Applications/XAMPP/htdocs/packt/bin/magento setup:cron:run
```

4. Run the `sudo crontab -u fjmiguel -l` command to take a look at your new cron job configuration.

5. Save the changes and exit the text editor.

In some cases, it is necessary to give write permissions again to the directories.

The `*/1 * * * *` configuration specifies that the cron job will be executed every minute. The cron job will now run in the background every minute. To manually execute the cron job, you can run the `php magento cron:run` command on the Magento command-line tool, as shown in the following figure:

```
MacBook-Pro:bin fjmiguel$ sudo crontab -u fjmiguel -e
crontab: installing new crontab
MacBook-Pro:bin fjmiguel$ sudo crontab -u fjmiguel -l
*/1 * * * * php -c /Applications/XAMPP/xamppfiles/etc/php.ini /Applications/XAMPP/
xamppfiles/etc/php.ini /Applications/XAMPP/htdocs/packt/bin/magento cron:run
*/1 * * * * php -c /Applications/XAMPP/xamppfiles/etc/php.ini /Applications/XAMPP/
xamppfiles/etc/php.ini /Applications/XAMPP/htdocs/packt/update/cron.php
*/1 * * * * php -c /Applications/XAMPP/xamppfiles/etc/php.ini /Applications/XAMPP/
htdocs/packt/bin/magento setup:cron:run
MacBook-Pro:bin fjmiguel$ php magento cron:run
Ran jobs by schedule.
You have mail in /var/mail/fjmiguel
```

For further information about the cron job, follow the link at `https://help.ubuntu.com/community/CronHowto`.

For Magento cron, take a look at the official Magento documentation `http://devdocs.magento.com/guides/v2.0/config-guide/cli/config-cli-subcommands-cron.html`.

Caching

While the indexing technique works on database layer, the caching feature does the same for the HTML page components to increase fast access to the frontend. Caching stores this kind of data in order to provide the visitors with access to faster download.

To enable caching, you need to perform the following steps:

1. Open the terminal or command prompt.
2. Access the `packt/bin` directory.
3. Run the `php magento cache:enable` command.

```
[MacBook-Pro:bin fjmiguel$ php magento cache:status
Current status:
                        config: 0
                        layout: 0
                    block_html: 0
                   collections: 0
                    reflection: 0
                        db_ddl: 0
                           eav: 0
            config_integration: 0
        config_integration_api: 0
                     full_page: 0
                     translate: 0
             config_webservice: 0
[MacBook-Pro:bin fjmiguel$ php magento cache:enable
Changed cache status:
                        config: 0 -> 1
                        layout: 0 -> 1
                    block_html: 0 -> 1
                   collections: 0 -> 1
                    reflection: 0 -> 1
                        db_ddl: 0 -> 1
                           eav: 0 -> 1
            config_integration: 0 -> 1
        config_integration_api: 0 -> 1
                     full_page: 0 -> 1
                     translate: 0 -> 1
             config_webservice: 0 -> 1
Cleaned cache types:
config
layout
block_html
collections
reflection
db_ddl
eav
config_integration
config_integration_api
full_page
translate
config_webservice
```

For further information about cache configuration, follow the link at `http://devdocs.magento.com/guides/v2.0/config-guide/cli/config-cli-subcommands-cache.html`.

You can work with third-party cache solutions to provide a better performance. Some of this solution has support and works very well with the Magento 2.0 solution. This book doesn't cover server configurations, but I strongly suggest you to take a look at the following:

- **Redis** can be found at `http://devdocs.magento.com/guides/v2.0/config-guide/redis/config-redis.html`
- **Memcached** session storage can be found at `http://devdocs.magento.com/guides/v2.0/config-guide/memcache/memcache.html`
- **Varnish** cache can be found at `http://devdocs.magento.com/guides/v2.0/config-guide/varnish/config-varnish.html`

Fine-tuning the Magento hosting server

Magento 2.0 has a complex structure, but it follows the good practices of software development, which gives the administrators and the developers of this fantastic e-commerce solution the real possibility to implement a scalable system to conquer a great site traffic and constantly increase the sales.

Despite this advantage, all the scalable systems need a great server infrastructure to provide fast content access through the Internet.

As a developer, you need to always think about all the stages that a successful software needs to go through in an order to aggregate the real value to its administrator and to its users. Try to always see the big picture of your project.

Let's take a look at some techniques and tips to increase your Magento server's capability.

Selecting the right Magento hosting service

First of all, we need to conduct a deep research on the existent solutions. We will try to gather information about clients of these solutions and test Magento's performance by accessing the Magento website as a visitor.

The Magento official project website provides you with an online tool to search for Magento. You can use this tool by accessing the URL at `http://partners.magento.com/partner_locator/search.aspx`.

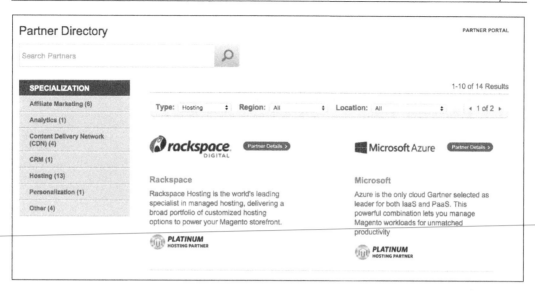

Apache web server deflation

Magento hosting services generally use Apache as a web server solution. Magento is written in PHP, and Apache has a mature environment to handle PHP processes.

In order to give fast response to visitors' requests, we will use Apache's `mod_deflate` to speed up server response.

According to Apache's official documentation (`http://httpd.apache.org/docs/2.2/mod/mod_deflate.html`), this module provides the `deflate` output filter that allows output from your server to be compressed before being sent to the client over the network.

To enable this feature on your server, you need to create the `.htaccess` file and enter the following code:

```
<IfModule mod_deflate.c>

###########################################
## enable apache served files compression
## http://developer.yahoo.com/performance/rules.html#gzip

    # Insert filter on all content
    SetOutputFilter DEFLATE
    # Insert filter on selected content types only
```

```
    AddOutputFilterByType DEFLATE text/html text/plain text/xml text/
css text/javascript

    # Netscape 4.x has some problems...
    BrowserMatch ^Mozilla/4 gzip-only-text/html

    # Netscape 4.06-4.08 have some more problems
    BrowserMatch ^Mozilla/4\.0[678] no-gzip

    # MSIE masquerades as Netscape, but it is fine
    BrowserMatch \bMSIE !no-gzip !gzip-only-text/html

    # Don't compress images
    SetEnvIfNoCase Request_URI \.(?:gif|jpe?g|png)$ no-gzip dont-vary

    # Make sure proxies don't deliver the wrong content
    Header append Vary User-Agent env=!dont-vary

</IfModule>
```

This adjustment reduces about 70% of the amount of data delivered.

For further information about the `.htaccess` and `mod_deflate` configurations, take a look at the links at `http://httpd.apache.org/docs/current/howto/htaccess.html` and `http://httpd.apache.org/docs/2.2/mod/mod_deflate.html`.

Enabling the expires header

Continuing to take advantage of the Apache web server, we will activate the `mod_expires` module. This module sends a message to the client machine about the document's validity, and the client can store a cache of the site until the client receives a new message from the server expiration of data. This technique increases the speed of download.

To activate this feature, you can open the `.htaccess` file available in the Magento root directory and enter this block of code:

```
<IfModule mod_expires.c>

############################################
## Add default Expires header
## http://developer.yahoo.com/performance/rules.html#expires

    ExpiresActive On
```

```
        ExpiresDefault "access plus 1 year"

    </IfModule>
```

For further information about the `.htaccess` configuration, follow the link at `http://httpd.apache.org/docs/2.2/mod/mod_expires.html`.

PHP memory configuration

Increasing PHP memory by host configuration has a direct relationship with your contracted hosting service. Some shared hosting services do not give this option to the developers. This is one of the main reasons to choose a specialized Magento hosting service.

Generally, this configuration can be done by adding the following code to the `.htaccess` file available in the Magento root directory:

```
    <IfModule mod_php5.c>

    #############################################
    ## adjust memory limit

    php_value memory_limit 256M
    php_value max_execution_time 18000

    </IfModule>
```

Optimizing the MySQL server

MySQL has the **query cache** feature to provide fast queries on a database. Once again, you need to conduct deep research on your possible hosting services before contracting any to make sure you have all the services you need for a great production environment.

Before starting the optimization, refer to the PHP and MySQL documentations of your hosting service to check the availability of these changes.

Open the `php.ini` hosting service file and place these configurations:

```
    ;;;;;;;;;;;;;;;;;;;
    ; Resource Limits ;
    ;;;;;;;;;;;;;;;;;;;

    max_execution_time = 30      ; Maximum execution time of each script,
    in seconds
```

```
max_input_time = 60      ; Maximum amount of time each script may spend
parsing request data
memory_limit = 512M        ; Maximum amount of memory a script may
consume (8MB)
query_cache_size = 64M


[MySQLi]
; Please refer to http://php.net/manual/en/mysqli.configuration.php
for further information

; Maximum number of persistent links.  -1 means no limit.
mysqli.max_persistent = -1

; Allow accessing, from PHP's perspective, local files with LOAD DATA
statements
;mysqli.allow_local_infile = On

; Allow or prevent persistent links.
mysqli.allow_persistent = On

; Maximum number of links.  -1 means no limit.
mysqli.max_links = -1

; If mysqlnd is used: Number of cache slots for the internal result
set cache
mysqli.cache_size = 2000

; Default port number for mysqli_connect().  If unset, mysqli_
connect() will use
; the $MYSQL_TCP_PORT or the mysql-tcp entry in /etc/services or the
; compile-time value defined MYSQL_PORT (in that order).  Win32 will
only look
; at MYSQL_PORT.
mysqli.default_port = 3306

; Default socket name for local MySQL connects.  If empty, uses the
built-in
; MySQL defaults.
mysqli.default_socket =

; Default host for mysql_connect() (doesn't apply in safe mode).
mysqli.default_host =

; Default user for mysql_connect() (doesn't apply in safe mode).
mysqli.default_user =

; Default password for mysqli_connect() (doesn't apply in safe mode).
; Note that this is generally a *bad* idea to store passwords in this
file.
```

```
; *Any* user with PHP access can run 'echo get_cfg_var("mysqli.
default_pw")
; and reveal this password!  And of course, any users with read access
to this
; file will be able to reveal the password as well.
mysqli.default_pw =

; Allow or prevent reconnect
mysqli.reconnect = Off
```

Now, let's configure the `query_cache_size` variable directly on the MySQL database.

Open the phpMyAdmin web SQL console, and execute the SHOW VARIABLES LIKE `'query_cache_size';` query without selecting a database. The query will probably return the 0 value for the `query_cache_size` variable.

Execute the SET GLOBAL `query_cache_size` = 1048576; query and execute SHOW VARIABLES LIKE `'query_cache_size';` again.

The query will probably return the following information:

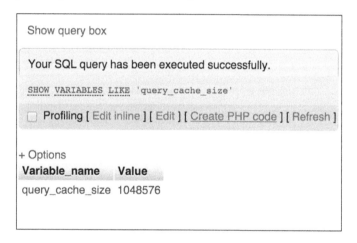

The `query_cache_size` variable was activated with success!

For further information about the MySQL cache size configuration, follow the link at `https://dev.mysql.com/doc/refman/5.0/en/query-cache-configuration.html`.

Even by testing these configurations in your localhost environment, you can feel the huge positive difference between the first access in your Magento installation and the last access after the configuration. This is really awesome!

Minifying scripts

Code minification is a technique to remove unnecessary characters from the source code. Minify your JavaScript (.js) and stylesheets (.css) files and improve the load time of your site by compressing the files.

In order to activate this process in Magento, navigate to the admin area (http://localhost/packt/admin_packt) and follow these instructions:

1. First, navigate to **Stores | Configuration | Advanced | Developer**.
2. Expand the **JavaScript Settings** options and select the **Yes** option for **Merge JavaScript Files** and **Minify JavaScript Files**.
3. Expand the **CSS Settings** options and select the **Yes** option for **Merge CSS Files** and **Minify CSS Files**.
4. Finally, click on the **Save Config** button.

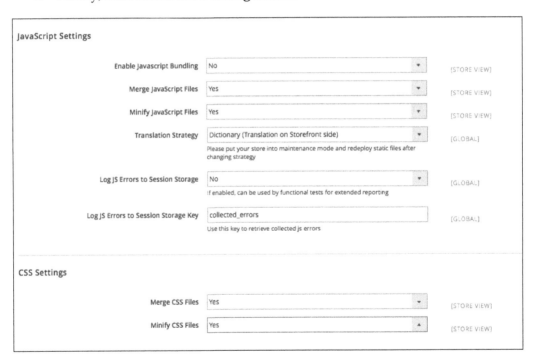

CDN for Magento

Content Delivery Networks, also known as **CDN**, are servers of fast access for your static or non-dynamic content. JavaScript files and images are examples of files hosted on CDN servers.

The main idea behind the use of CDN is saving the process time of your Magento server using a CDN solution.

I suggest you to conduct research on hosting services that provide this integration. For example, **Nexcess** as a Magento partner company provides specific documentation about CDN integration on the URL `https://docs.nexcess.net/article/how-to-configure-cdn-access-for-magento.html`.

For JavaScript CDN, we have a free-of-charge service available on the Internet! This is thanks to Google for providing us with this amazing feature at `https://developers.google.com/speed/libraries/`.

Summary

In this chapter, you learned important lessons about how to improve Magento performance and pay attention to all the aspects that can make a positive difference in Magento development, including how to create a full-speed environment for Magento System.

I invite you to think in this very for now. We are progressing and walking through all the aspects of Magento: design, development, marketing, and performance. I feel comfortable to say to you, dear reader, that you have the tools to elevate your Magento professional career. Just keep continuing to study hard.

In this chapter, you learned how to:

- Increase Magento performance in different aspects and technologies
- Use the power of indexation and caching
- Develop solutions to create a better Magento user experience through fast download techniques

In the final chapter, we will explore some tools and ways to improve your Magento skills. See you!

9
Improving Your Magento Skills

We are at the end of the book, but this only the beginning of your walk through the Magento training. It's important to know some Magento extension options, but it is more important to build your own path in the Magento world by studying for a certification and achieving a new professional level.

The following topics will be covered in this chapter:

- Magento Connect extensions
- Installing a Magento extension
- Debugging Grunt.js styles
- Magento knowledge center
- Improving your Magento skills

Magento Connect extensions

The Magento 2.0 architecture allows a natural improvement of native resources and the addition of new ones. Magento 2.0 is built based on the best software development practices. Its architecture is modular, which allows the development of extensions, as we discussed in an earlier chapter.

Magento Commerce maintains a marketplace to provide Magento extensions known as **Magento Connect** (`https://www.magentocommerce.com/magento-connect`). Magento Connect includes extensions that provide new functionalities, such as modules, add-ons, language packs, design interfaces, and themes to extend the power of your store.

I strongly suggest that you visit Magento Connect to get some ideas for personal projects and follow the extension development tendency in the marketplace.

Installing a Magento extension

Besides the Magento Connect marketplace, to search for Magento extension solutions, you can access the extension options through your admin area. To access Magento extension options in your admin area, perform the following steps:

1. Access your admin area at `http://localhost/admin_packt`.

2. Navigate to **Find Partners and Extensions | Visit Magento Marketplaces**.

3. Once you choose the extension to install, Magento 2.0 offers two options for extension installation:

   ° Installation via Composer

   ° Manual installation

To install the extensions via Composer, you need to configure `composer.json` to work with the **Magento 2 Composer** repository (`http://packages.magento.com/`) as a repository solution for **Magento Core** extensions. The composer already has the **Packagist** (`https://packagist.org/`) configuration. To proceed with this configuration, perform the following:

1. Open the terminal or command prompt.
2. Go to the root directory of your Magento installation.
3. Run the `composer config repositories.magento composer http://packages.magento.com` command.

To install a Magento extension via `composer`, do the following:

1. Open the terminal or command prompt.
2. Go to the root directory of your Magento installation.
3. Run the `composer require <vendor>/<module>` command.
4. An example of this is `composer require Packt/TweetsAbout`.
5. Run the `composer update` command.
6. Then, run the `php bin/magento setup:upgrade` command.
7. In some cases, it is necessary to give write permissions again to the directories.

To install a Magento extension manually, perform the following steps:

1. Download the `.zip` file of the module.
2. Extract it and move it under the `<magento_root_directory>/app/code` directory.
3. Run the `php bin/magento setup:upgrade` command.
4. In some cases, it is necessary to give write permissions again to the directories (for example, the `var` directory)

Debugging styles with the Grunt task runner

As you noted in the previous chapters, for every change that you apply in a Magento extension or theme styles, you need to clean the static files directory and deploy it to see the effect. This process takes time and unnecessary effort. So, what if you have a tool to automate this process?

Grunt.js (http://gruntjs.com/) is a task runner to automate tasks; for example, it provides productivity in Magento development by automating CSS changes. To install Grunt, follow these steps:

1. Install **Node.js** (https://nodejs.org) in your machine.

2. Open the terminal or command prompt.

3. Run the `npm install -g grunt-cli` command to install the Grunt command-line interface.

4. Go to the `packt/` Magento root directory and run the `npm install grunt --save-dev` command.

5. Still under the `packt` directory, run the `npm install` command.

6. Then, run the `npm update` command.

7. In your favorite code editor open, the `packt/dev/tools/grunt/configs/theme.js` file, add the following code, and save it:

    ```
    'use strict';

    module.exports = {
        blank: {
            area: 'frontend',
            name: 'Magento/blank',
            locale: 'en_US',
            files: [
                'css/styles-m',
                'css/styles-l',
                'css/email',
                'css/email-inline'
            ],
            dsl: 'less'
        },
        luma: {
            area: 'frontend',
            name: 'Magento/luma',
            locale: 'en_US',
            files: [
                'css/styles-m',
                'css/styles-l'
            ],
    ```

```
            dsl: 'less'
        },
        backend: {
            area: 'adminhtml',
            name: 'Magento/backend',
            locale: 'en_US',
            files: [
                'css/styles-old',
                'css/styles'
            ],
            dsl: 'less'
        },

        compstore: {
            area: 'frontend',
            name: 'Packt/compstore',
            locale: 'en_US',
            files: [
              'css/styles-m',
              'css/styles-l',
              'css/source/compstore'
            ],
            dsl: 'less'
        }
    };
```

Once the Grunt environment is configured, it's time to test Grunt. Perform the following steps:

1. Open the terminal or command prompt.
2. Run the `grunt exec:compstore` command.
3. Then, run the `grunt less:compstore` command.

4. Run the `grunt watch` command.

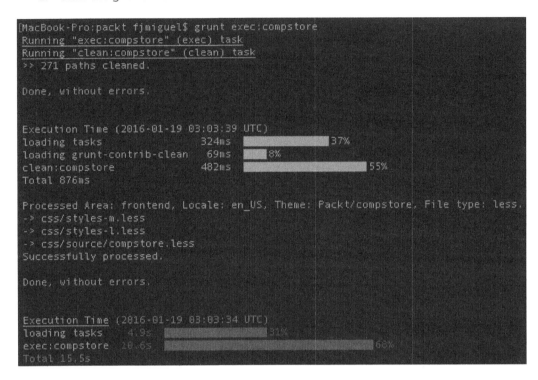

These commands will create a direct channel with the possibility to edit your `.css` files on the fly. The `grunt watch` command shows you the update in real time. With "grunt watch" still active in your terminal/prompt window, try to edit and save the body's background color in the `app/design/frontend/Packt/compstore/web/css/source/compstore.less` file to see the result in the browser by accessing your base URL:

```
MacBook-Pro:packt fjmiguel$ grunt watch
Running "watch" task
Waiting...
>> File "pub/static/frontend/Packt/compstore/en_US/css/source/compstore.less" chan
ged.
Running "less:compstore" (less) task
File pub/static/frontend/Packt/compstore/en_US/css/styles-m.css created: 329.1 kB
→ 565.36 kB
File pub/static/frontend/Packt/compstore/en_US/css/styles-l.css created: 97.37 kB
→ 166.79 kB
File pub/static/frontend/Packt/compstore/en_US/css/source/compstore.css created: 3
2 B → 269 B

Done, without errors.


Execution Time (2016-01-19 03:18:34 UTC)
loading tasks            345ms    3%
loading grunt-contrib-less  704ms    5%
less:compstore           12.7s           92%
Total 13.7s

Completed in 14.344s at Tue Jan 19 2016 01:18:47 GMT-0200 (BRST) - Waiting...
>> File "pub/static/frontend/Packt/compstore/en_US/css/styles-m.css" changed.
>> File "pub/static/frontend/Packt/compstore/en_US/css/source/compstore.css" chang
ed.
>> File "pub/static/frontend/Packt/compstore/en_US/css/styles-l.css" changed.
Completed in 0.001s at Tue Jan 19 2016 01:18:48 GMT-0200 (BRST) - Waiting...
```

Magento knowledge center

The Magento team provides great resources of documentation in order to increase the Magento developer's knowledge.

In the Magento documentation (http://magento.com/help/documentation), the user can access the **USER GUIDES** section for **ENTERPRISE EDITION**, **COMMUNITY EDITION**, **DESIGNER'S GUIDE**, and **DEVELOPER DOCUMENTATION**.

I strongly suggest that you, dear reader, study Magento's **COMMUNITY EDITION, DESIGNER'S GUIDE**, and **DEVELOPER DOCUMENTATION** in the first instance. These three documentations have solid concepts, and you can certainly take advantage by building your Magento concepts.

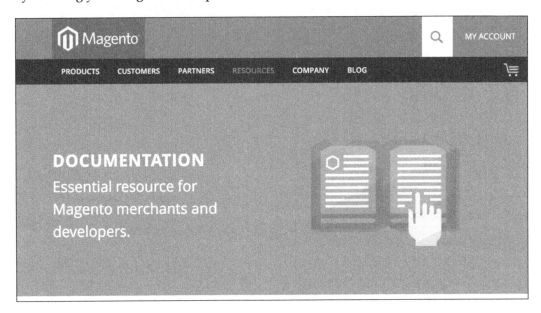

Improving your Magento skills

Welcome to the world of information technology! The professionals of this area need to study harder every single day. It's totally crazy how technology is always in mutation. New technologies and solutions come in a short period of time, and professionals must be prepared all the time to keep an open mind, absorbing this situation assertively.

Magento provides an official training program available at `http://magento.com/training/overview`. You can access information about courses, and I strongly suggest that you think about **Magento certification**. Certifications can boost your career.

To learn more about Magento certification, refer to `http://magento.com/training/catalog/certification`. You can download a free Magento study guide by visiting `http://magento.com/training/free-study-guide`.

You have a lot of options, such as books, articles, and blogs, to train and improve your Magento skills. Be persistent on your objectives!

Summary

Congratulations! You won one more challenge; first, you acquired this great book, and then you completed the reading with merits. It was not easy, but I'm certain it was worth it.

In this chapter, you learned how to:

- Manage Magento extensions
- Test some Magento extension options
- Build your own path to become a Magento success professional

Thank you so much. I know you can climb the highest mountains; never lose faith in yourself. Good luck!

Index

Symbols

.htaccess configuration
  reference link 132
.json format
  reference link 64

A

aheadWorks
  URL 8
Apache
  about 2
  URL 2
Apache Friends 2
Apache Friends Support Forum
  URL 4
Apache Varnish 16
Apache Web server deflation
  about 131, 132
  reference link 131
Application Programming Interface
        (API) 16
Atom.io 51, 52

B

basic Magento 2.0 theme
  creating 50
Bitnami
  URL 4
blank theme features 45
blocks 90, 91
bundler
  URL 60

C

cache configuration
  reference link 129
cache management
  about 50
  reference link 24
caching
  about 125
  enabling 128, 129
CDN 137
CDN for Magento 137
Chrome Web Store
  URL 108
CMS blocks 47
CMS pages 47
command-line configuration,
        Magento 2.0 22
command-line utility 22-24
Community Edition (CE) 7
Composer
  about 60, 61
  installing, on Unix-like operating
        systems 61
  URL 60
composer.json file, parameters
  autoload 64
  description 64
  license 64
  name 64
  require 64
  type 64
  version 64
Composer packages
  reference link 86

X

XAMPP
  about 2
  installing 3
  installing, for Linux 6
  installing, for OS X 7
  installing, for Windows 3-5
  URL 3
XAMPP PHP development environment 2

Z

Zend framework
  URL 13
  using 78
Zend framework Case Study
  reference link 78

Thank you for buying
Magento 2 Development Essentials

About Packt Publishing

Packt, pronounced 'packed', published its first book, *Mastering phpMyAdmin for Effective MySQL Management*, in April 2004, and subsequently continued to specialize in publishing highly focused books on specific technologies and solutions.

Our books and publications share the experiences of your fellow IT professionals in adapting and customizing today's systems, applications, and frameworks. Our solution-based books give you the knowledge and power to customize the software and technologies you're using to get the job done. Packt books are more specific and less general than the IT books you have seen in the past. Our unique business model allows us to bring you more focused information, giving you more of what you need to know, and less of what you don't.

Packt is a modern yet unique publishing company that focuses on producing quality, cutting-edge books for communities of developers, administrators, and newbies alike. For more information, please visit our website at www.packtpub.com.

About Packt Open Source

In 2010, Packt launched two new brands, Packt Open Source and Packt Enterprise, in order to continue its focus on specialization. This book is part of the Packt Open Source brand, home to books published on software built around open source licenses, and offering information to anybody from advanced developers to budding web designers. The Open Source brand also runs Packt's Open Source Royalty Scheme, by which Packt gives a royalty to each open source project about whose software a book is sold.

Writing for Packt

We welcome all inquiries from people who are interested in authoring. Book proposals should be sent to author@packtpub.com. If your book idea is still at an early stage and you would like to discuss it first before writing a formal book proposal, then please contact us; one of our commissioning editors will get in touch with you.

We're not just looking for published authors; if you have strong technical skills but no writing experience, our experienced editors can help you develop a writing career, or simply get some additional reward for your expertise.

Magento 2 Developer's Guide

ISBN: 978-1-78588-658-4   Paperback: 412 pages

Harness the power of Magento 2, the most recent version of the world's favorite e-commerce platform, for your online store

1. Set up, configure, and power up your Magento environment from development to production.

2. Master the use of Web API to communicate with the Magento system and create custom services .

3. Create custom modules from scratch to extend the core functionality of the Magento system.

Magento 2 Development Cookbook

ISBN: 978-1-78588-219-7   Paperback: 304 pages

Over 60 recipes that will tailor and customize your experience with Magento 2

1. Solve common problems encountered while extending your Magento 2 store to fit your business needs.

2. Delve into the exciting and enhanced features of Magento 2 such as customizing security permissions, intelligent filtered search options, easy third-party integration, among others.

3. Learn to build and maintain a Magento 2 shop via a visual-based page editor and customize the look and feel using Magento 2's offerings on the go.

Please check **www.PacktPub.com** for information on our titles

open source
community experience distilled

Mastering Magento Theme Design

ISBN: 978-1-78328-823-6   Paperback: 310 pages

Create responsive Magento themes using Bootstrap, the most widely used frontend framework

1. Create an advanced responsive Magento theme based on the framework Bootstrap 3.

2. Create a powerful admin theme options panel.

3. Loaded with practical live coding example to create the theme from scratch.

Learning Magento Theme Development

ISBN: 978-1-78328-061-2   Paperback: 182 pages

Create visually stunning and responsive themes to customize the appearance of your Magento store

1. Create a custom theme from scratch for your Magento store.

2. Change the basics of your Magento theme from the logo of your store to the color scheme of your theme.

3. Easy-to-follow step-by-step guide on how to get up and running with Magento themes.

Please check **www.PacktPub.com** for information on our titles

Lightning Source UK Ltd.
Milton Keynes UK
UKOW07f2217210316

270611UK00001B/43/P